Contents

Study Guide to y

ONE WEEKssion ef

eventh Edition.

Study Guide to Accompany

The Professional Chef
Seventh Edition

The Culinary Institute of America

JOHN WILEY & SONS, INC.

Published by John Wiley & Sons, Inc.

Published simultaneously in Canada.

This publication is designed to provide accurate and authoritative information in regard to the subject matter covered. It is sold with the understanding that the publisher is not engaged in rendering professional services. If professional advice or other expert assistance is required, the services of a competent professional person should be sought.

This material may be reproduced for testing or instructional purposes by instructors using the text *The Professional Chef, Seventh Edition*, by The Culinary Institute of America (ISBN: 0-471-38257-4).

Library of Congress Cataloging-in-Publication Data:

ISBN: 0-471-20916-3

Printed in the United States of America.

10 9 8 7 6 5 4 3

CHAPTER 1

Chapter Overview

A culinarian is a member of a profession with a fascinating history. Knowing where you have come from may be the best way to appreciate the choices, responsibilities, and opportunities that await you as a professional chef.

Chapter Objectives

After reading and studying this chapter, you will be able to:

➢ name some key events, people, and books important in culinary history

➢ identify a variety of career opportunities and describe them

➢ list a number of different types of foodservice establishments

➢ explain the background and importance of a kitchen and dining room brigade system

➢ name a variety of other opportunities in culinary careers

➢ describe the paths to becoming a professional culinarian through education, experience, networking, and continuing education

➢ define the attributes of a culinarian

➢ identify a number of challenges facing today's culinarians

Study Outline

Restaurant History and Evolution

Key Terms and Concepts

cuisine classique (classic or classical cuisine)

French revolution

fusion cuisine

grande cuisine

nouvelle cuisine

restaurant

table d'hôte

Career Opportunities for Culinary Professionals

Key Terms and Concepts

banquet
bistro
cafeteria
caterers
coffee shop
executive dining room
family-style restaurant
fast-food outlets

fine-dining restaurant
food service
full-service restaurant
grill
home meal replacement
 (carry out)
hotels
institutional catering

on-site services
off-site services
private club
room service
white-tablecloth
 establishment/restaurant

The Kitchen Brigade System

Key Terms and Concepts

aboyeur
announcer
apprentice
boucher
boulanger
brigade system
butcher
chef
chef de cuisine
cold-foods chef
commis
communard
confiseur
décorateur

entremetier
executive chef
expeditier
family meal
fish chef
friturier
fry chef
garde-manger
glacier
grill chef
grillardin
legumier
pantry chef
pastry chef

pâtissier
poissonier
potager
roast chef
rôtisseur
roundsman
saucier
sauté chef
sous chef
station
tournant
vegetable chef

Brigade Positions – Kitchen

chef (*chef de cuisine/executive chef*)
sous chef
sauté chef (*saucier*)
fish chef (*poissonier*)
roast chef (*rôtisseur*)
grill chef (*grillardin*)
fry chef (*friturier*)
vegetable chef (*entremetier/potager/
 legumier*)

roundsman (*tournant/swing cook*)
cold-foods chef (garde-manger/pantry chef)
butcher (*boucher*)
pastry chef
 (*pâtissier/confiseur/boulanger/glacier/
 décorateur*)
expediter/announcer (*aboyeur*)
communard
apprentice/*commis*

The Dining Room Brigade System

Key Terms and Concept

back waiter
busboy
captain
chef d'étage
chef de rang
chef de salle
chef de vin
commis de rang

demi-chef de rang
dining room (not in brigade list)
dining room manager
front-of-the-house (not in brigade list)
front waiter
headwaiter

maître d'hôtel
sommelier
tableside food preparation (not in brigade list)
wine list (not in brigade list)
wine steward

Brigade Positions – Dining Room

dining room manager (*maître d'hôtel*)
wine steward (*chef de vin/sommelier*)
headwaiter (*chef de salle*)
captain (*chef d'étage*)

front waiter (*chef de rang*)
back waiter/busboy (*demi-chef de rang* or *commis de rang*)

Other Opportunities

Key Terms and Concepts

consultant
design specialist
food and beverage manager
food critic
food photographer
food stylist
food writer
research-and-development kitchen
salesperson

teacher
food and beverage managers
consultants and design specialists
well-informed salespeople
teachers
food writers and critics
food stylists and photographers
research-and-development kitchens

Becoming a Culinary Professional

Formal education and training

Key Terms and Concepts

accredited school
apprenticeship program
culinary education

formal training
hands-on practice
on-the-job training

self-directed course of study
theory

Continuing Education

Key Terms and Concepts

classes

continuing education

culinary professionals

professional organization

seminar

workshop

Networking

Key Terms and Concepts

business cards

professional network

trade shows

The Attributes of a Culinary Professional

Key Terms and Concepts

appreciation of quality

commitment to service

customer

dedication to quality

judgement

open and inquiring mind

sense of responsibility

The Chef as Businessperson

Key Terms and Concepts

accounting system

administrator

budget

customer complaint

executive

food cost

human resources

information

inventory

inventory control system

losses

manager

mission/plan

payroll

physical assets

profit

purchases

reservations

sales

schedule

software

time

Become a good executive.

Become a good administrator.

Become a good manager.

Managing Physical Assets

Key Terms and Concepts

computers
equipment and supplies
expenses

food and beverage inventory
point-of-sale systems
purchasing agent

purchasing system
ware-washing machines

Managing Information

Managing Human Resources

Key Terms and Concepts

access to potable water and
    bathroom facilities
constructive criticism
disability insurance
disciplinary measures
employee benefits package
environment free from
    physical hazards

feedback
I-9 form
Immigration and
    Naturalization Service
    (INS)
job description
legal deductions
legal responsibilities

liability insurance
objective evaluation
report all earnings
team effort
training
unemployment insurance
worker's compensation

Managing time

Invest time in reviewing daily operations.
Invest time in training others.
Learn to communicate clearly.

Take steps to create an orderly work
environment.
Purchase, replace, and maintain all necessary
tools

The Challenges of the Restaurant Industry

Key Terms and Concepts

customer service
facility management
marketing

Chapter 1 Exercises

True/False

Indicate whether each of the following statements is True (T) or False (F)

_____ 1. The French revolution played an important part in restaurant proliferation because French chefs won the right to open their own restaurants.

_____ 2. In the classic brigade system, the communard is responsible for preparing the meal served to the staff (also known as family meal).

_____ 3. One reason the role of expediter or announcer is important is because that person is the last to see the plate before it leaves the kitchen.

_____ 4. *Physiologie de goût* (*The Physiology of Taste*) was written by Georges-Auguste Escoffier.

_____ 5. The code established in *le guide culinaire* was replaced by a more refined and simplified approach to cooking referred to as the *grande cuisine*.

_____ 6. The *grande cuisine* was well suited to royal and noble households but difficult to maintain in hotel kitchens at the time it was created.

_____ 7. *Fusion cuisine* was a cooking style defined by Fernand Point and his disciples.

_____ 8. The brigade system was developed to streamline work in hotel kitchens and is rarely used in independent restaurants.

_____ 9. If human resources are managed correctly, there is never a need to take disciplinary measures.

_____ 10. A food and beverage manager is responsible for all food and beverage outlets in a hotel or other large food service establishment.

Multiple Choice

1. The original code established by Marie-Antoine Carême that detailed numerous dishes and their sauces suited to royal and noble households is known as
   a. grande cuisine.
   b. nouvelle cuisine.
   c. cuisine classique.

d. brigade system.

2. The code established by Escoffier that produced a more refined and simplified approach to cooking technique that is still in use today is known as
   a. grande cuisine.
   b. nouvelle cuisine.
   c. cuisine classique.
   d. brigade system.

3. The practice instituted by Escoffier to streamline and simplify work in hotel kitchens is known as
   a. station system.
   b. back of the house.
   c. inventory control system.
   d. brigade system.

4. The French chefs known as the *Bande à Bocuse* are credited with inventing
   a. *grande cuisine.*
   b. nouvelle cuisine.
   c. *cuisine classique.*
   d. fusion cuisine.

5. The person responsible for accepting orders from the dining room and relaying them to the various station chefs is the
   a. commis.
   b. roundsman.
   c. pantry chef.
   d. expediter.

Fill in the Blank

1. _____was the Florentine princess who introduced a more refined style of dining to France and whose chefs influenced French chefs as well.

2. _____was a member of a royal Spanish family whose chefs introduced sauce espagnole and the use of roux to France.

3. _____was the author of *Le Vrai Cuisinier François*, published in 1651.

4. _____ was a French politician, gourmet, and the author of *Physiologie de goût.*

5. The "chef of kings, king of chefs" _____ was known as the founder of grande cuisine and was responsible for systemizing culinary techniques.

Matching

_____ 1. poissonier

_____ 2. tournant

_____ 3. chef de salle

_____ 4. entremetier

_____ 5. boucher

_____ 6. maitre d'hôtel

a. head waiter

b. roundsman

c. dining room manager

d. butcher

e. fish chef

f. vegetable chef

Written/Short Answer

1. Briefly explain *grande cuisine*, *cuisine classique*, and nouvelle cuisine.

_____

_____

_____

_____

2. What kitchen or cooking positions are available to the trained culinary professional?

_____

_____

_____

_____

3. What is networking, why, and how is it done?

_____

_____

_____

_____

4. In addition to kitchen positions, what other career opportunities are available for the trained and educated culinary professional?

_____

_____

_____

_____

5. Discuss the three primary attributes of the culinary professional (discussed in the text).

_____

_____

_____

_____

CHAPTER 2

MENUS AND RECIPES

Chapter Overview

Menus are used in the dining room to give both wait staff and guests important information about what the establishment offers. Recipes give detailed instructions to aid kitchen staff in producing menu items. But, more than that, carefully designed menus and comprehensive recipes can help the professional chef streamline kitchen operations and control costs.

Chapter Objectives

After reading and studying this chapter, you will be able to:

➤ list several types of menus and describe them

➤ explain what is meant by a standardized recipe

➤ name the elements in a standard recipe and how they are used as effective business and management tools in the operation of a professional kitchen

➤ measure dry and liquid ingredients properly

➤ increase and decrease (also known as "scale") recipes to suit production needs using appropriate formulas and calculations

➤ use basic recipe and yield calculations to determine food and recipe costs

➤ convert from one measurement system to another properly

Study Outline

Menus

Key Terms and Concepts

menu	banquet menu	menu pricing strategy
à la carte menu	menu development	plate/plating

Recipes

Key Terms and Concepts

accurate measurements
consistency of quality
consistency of quantity
computerized database
count
critical control points (CCPs)
decreasing the yield
holding

increasing the yield
mise en place
plating information
portion size
published recipe
recipe
recipe conversion
recipe management program

recipe modification
serving
standardized recipes
volume
weight
yield

Basic Method

Measuring Ingredients Accurately

Basic Method

Standardized Recipes

Name/title of the food item or dish
Yield information for the recipe
Portion information for each serving
Ingredient names
Ingredient measures
Ingredient preparation instructions

Equipment information
Preparation steps
Service information
Holding and reheating procedures
Critical control points (CCPs)

Recipe Calculations

Key Terms and Concepts

as-purchased cost (APC)
as-purchased quantity (APQ)
common unit of measure
cost per unit
decimal system
decrease the portion size
decrease the yield
edible portion cost (EPC)
edible portion quantity (EPQ)
fluid ounces
increase the portion size
increase the yield
metric measurement system
price per pound (each, dozen, quart, etc.)
purchase pack price
purchase units
raw product

recipe conversion
recipe conversion factor
recipe modification
scale
scaling ingredients
scaling up or down
tare
testing the recipe
trim loss
unit price
U.S. measurement system
usable trim
wholesale bulk size
wholesome trim
yield percentage
yield test

Basic Method: Using a Recipe Conversion Factor (RCT) to convert recipe yields

CONVERSION FORMULA

Basic Method: Converting portion sizes

CONVERSION FORMULA

Basic Method: Converting volume measures to weight

CONVERSION INSTRUCTIONS

Basic Method: Converting between U.S. and metric measurement systems

CONVERSION FORMULAS

METRIC PREFIXES

Basic Method: Converting to a common unit of measure

COMMON CONVERSION CHART

Basic Method: Calculating as-purchased cost (APC)

APC FORMULA

Basic method: Calculating the yield of fresh fruits and vegetables and determining yield percentage

YIELD PERCENTAGE FORMULA

Basic method: Calculating the as-purchased (APQ) using yield percentage

APQ FORMULA

Basic method: Calculating edible portion quantity (EPQ) using yield percentage

EPQ FORMULA

Basic method: Calculating edible portion cost

EPC FORMULA

Basic method: Calculating the value of usable trim

VALUE OF USABLE TRIM FORMULA

Using Recipes Effectively

Key concepts and terms

decrease food cost   improve organization   reduce loss
improve efficiency   increase profits

Chapter 2 Exercises

True/False

Indicate whether each of the following statesments is True (T) or False (F)

_____ 1. The purpose of the butcher's yield test is to determine how many portions can be fabricated from meat, fish, or poultry.

_____ 2. When preparing fruits and vegetables for a fruit salad, the particular cut or size that the chef chooses might affect the amount of trim loss.

_____ 3. When performing a butcher's yield test, if bones have a use in the kitchen they may be included in the calculations of trim value.

_____ 4. Yield percentage on any given food item may vary depending on the intended use of that item.

_____ 5. The value of beef tenderloin fillet trim used to make ground beef would be the same as the price you paid for the tenderloin.

_____ 6. The value of boneless chicken trim used to make ground chicken would be the same as the price you have to pay to purchase ground chicken.

_____ 7. To determine how many portions are in a case, you must determine the edible portion quantity and then divide that by the portion size, using a common unit of measure.

_____ 8. Many refined foods such as flour and sugar have a yield percentage of 100 percent.

_____ 9. When a recipe is converted to increase or decrease the total yield, the amount of all food items should be increased or decreased in the same proportion.

_____ 10 Most modern measuring equipment is capable of measuring both U.S. and metric units.

Multiple Choice

1. The recipe conversion factor is determined by
    a. dividing the edible portion quantity by the as-purchased quantity.
    b. dividing the as-purchased quantity by the edible portion quantity.
    c. dividing the desired yield by the original yield.
    d. dividing the original yield by the desired yield.

2. The recipe conversion factor is used to
    a. convert a recipe from metric to U.S. measurements.
    b. convert measures within a recipe from volume to weight or weight to volume.
    c. adjust the yield of a recipe to make more or less.
    d. convert all ingredients to a common unit of measure.

3. The calculation used to adjust the yield of a recipe to make either more or less is
    a. divide the desired yield by the original yield and multiply all ingredients by that number.
    b. determine the desired yield and multiply all ingredients by that number.
    c. divide the original yield by the desired yield and multiply all ingredients by that number.
    d. divide the as-purchased quantity by the edible portion quantity and multiply all ingredients by that number.

4. Before you can modify the portion size of a recipe, you will need to calculate
    a. the yield percentage.
    b. the total original yield and the total desired yield.
    c. the desired portion size minus the original portion size.
    d. the original portion size minus the desired portion size.

5. The yield percentage of an item is determined by
    a. dividing the edible portion quantity by the as-purchased quantity.
    b. dividing the as-purchased quantity by the edible portion quantity.
    c. dividing the desired yield by the original yield.
    d. dividing the original yield by the desired yield.

Fill in the Blank

1. To determine the as-purchased cost per unit, you must divide the _____ by the_____.

2. To adjust the yield of a recipe to make either more or less, you determine the _____ and multiply all the ingredients by that amount.

3. A _____ is done to find the accurate costs of fabricated meat, fish, and poultry.

4. The _____ is determined by dividing edible portion quantity by as-purchased quantity.

5. _____are important guidelines within recipe indicating temperatures and times for safe food handling procedures.

Matching

_____ 1. as-purchased cost

_____ 2. yield test

_____ 3. critical control points

_____ 4. edible portion quantity

_____ 5. tare

_____ 6. scaling

a. cut, trim, and weigh an item to determine yield percentage

b. wholesale price of item

c. weight of a container that is deducted when the container is filled and weighed

d. established safe temperatures for stages of recipe preparation

e. increasing or decreasing the amount of a recipe

f. as-purchased quantity x yield percentage

Written/Short Answer

1. Explain the different measuring conventions and when are they best used.

_____

_____

_____

_____

2. When increasing or decreasing the yield of a recipe, what must be considered?

_____

_____

_____

_____

3. How can you convert volume measure to weight measure?

_____

_____

_____

_____

4. Explain how to use or convert the metric system in U.S. kitchens.

_____

_____

_____

5. Why do measurements need to be converted to a common unit and how is it done for the U.S. measuring system?

_____

_____

_____

_____

CHAPTER 3

THE BASICS OF NUTRITION AND FOOD SCIENCE

Chapter Overview

The American people have become increasingly aware of the fact that good nutrition plays an important part in maintaining physical health and overall well-being. Consequently, culinary professionals must be aware of the nutritional content of their dishes. They must also understand the chemical and physical changes that occur when food is cooked.

Chapter Objectives

After reading and studying this chapter, you will be able to:

➢ define nutrition and the role of the following:

➢ calories, carbohydrates, fiber, fat, cholesterol, protein, water, vitamins and minerals, phytochemicals, and antioxidants

➢ explain what is meant by Dietary Guidelines and Recommendations

➢ describe the similarities and differences between 3 food guide pyramids (The USDA food guide pyramid, the Mediterranean Pyramid, and the Vegetarian Pyramid

➢ describe the effect on foods as they cook for each of following methods of heat transfer: conduction, convection, and radiation

➢ list the effects of heat on starches and sugars (caramelization, Maillard reaction, and gelatinization

➢ explain how denaturing proteins affects foods as they cook

➢ define the function of cooking fats

➢ name and describe the states of and function of water in cooking

➢ name the types of emulsions and how they are formed

➢ discuss the importance of nutrition and food science to the professional chef

Study Outline

Nutrition

Calories

Key Terms and Concepts

alcohol
calories
carbohydrates
energy

fat
kilocalories
nutrients
nutrient-dense

proteins
United States Department of
   Agriculture (USDA)

Carbohydrates

Key Terms and Concepts

complex carbohydrates
complex sugars
fat metabolism

fructose
glucose
lactose

simple sugars
sucrose
simple carbohydrates

Fiber

Key Terms and Concepts

cullulose
hemicelluloses
high serum cholesterol level

insoluble fiber
lignin
non-nutritive

soluble fiber

Fat

Key Terms and Concepts

coronary artery disease
digestion
fat soluble vitamins
fatty acids
Food and Drug
   Administration (FDA)

hydrogenated fat
monounsaturated fat
obesity
omega-3 fatty acids
polyunsaturated fat
satiety

saturated fat
serum cholesterol level
single fat
trans fat

Cholesterol

Key Terms and Concepts

dietary cholesterol

high-density lipoproteins
   (HDL)

low-density lipoproteins
   (LDL)

serum/blood cholesterol   sterol
serum cholesterol level   lipids

Protein

Key Terms and Concepts

amino acids   complete protein   mutual supplementation
combining complementary   eight essential amino acids
proteins   incomplete protein

Water

Vitamins and Minerals

Key Terms and Concepts

antioxidant   fat-soluble vitamins   macrominerals
Daily Values (DV)   free radicals   microminerals
electrolytes   noncaloric nutrient   water-soluble vitamins

Phytochemicals and Antioxidants

Key Terms and Concepts

antioxidants
free radicals
phytochemicals

Dietary Guidelines and Recommendations

The USDA food guide pyramid

Key Terms and Concepts

daily food allowances   number of recommended   recommended serving size
four food groups   servings   USDA Food Guide Pyramid
                               percentage of daily calories

The Mediterranean Pyramid

Key Terms and Concepts

Mediterranean diet
Oldways Preservation & Exchange Trust

The Vegetarian Pyramid

Key Terms and Concepts

vegan diet
vegetarian diet

Food Science Basics

Heat Transfer

Conduction
Convection
Radiation

Key Terms and Concepts

cooking
conduction
convection

infrared radiation
mechanical convection
microwave

radiation

Induction Cooking

Effects of Heat on Starches and Sugars: Caramelization, Maillard Reaction, and Gelatinization

Key Terms and Concepts

amino acids
caramelize/caramelization
gelatinization

Maillard reaction
starch
sugar

thickening properties

Denaturing Proteins

Key Terms and Concepts

denature/denaturing
denatured proteins

Function of Cooking Fats

Key Terms and Concepts

animal fats
liquid fats

solid fats
smoke point

vegetable oils

States of and Function of Water in Cooking

Key Terms and Concepts

acidic/acidity
alkaline/alkalinity
evaporate

freeze
pH
reduction

steam
water vapor

Forming Emulsions

Key Terms and Concepts

continuous phase
dispersed phase
emulsifiers

emulsion
oil-in-water emulsion
temporary emulsion

water-in-oil emulsion

The Importance of Nutrition and Food Science to the Professional Chef

Chapter 3 Exercises

True/False

Indicate whether each of the following statements is True (T) or False (F)

_____ 1. Iodized salt was introduced in the United States in the early 1900's to combat a growing deficiency in iron.

_____ 2. The B-complex vitamins are found only in animal foods, so vegetarians need to take supplements of these vitamins, or eat foods fortified with them.

_____ 3. The human body generally loses about one quart of water daily through the cleansing and cooling processes.

_____ 4. The microwave oven is used for conduction cooking, or the direct transfer of heat between adjacent molecules.

_____ 5. The caramelization process of granulated white sugar begins at 338°F/170°C.

_____ 6. Denatured proteins are more difficult to digest than natural proteins. The addition of fiber will assist in their digestion.

_____ 7. Solid shortening and margarine are two of the main sources of trans fat in the American diet and should be consumed in small amounts.

_____ 8. Convection heating is the transfer of heat through gases or liquids.

_____ 9. It is not essential to consume cholesterol because humans produce it from other dietary components.

_____ 10. Cholesterol is not the same thing as a cooking fat or animal fat, rather it is a fat-related compound.

Multiple Choice

1. Calories come from which four sources?
    a. Fats, alcohol, proteins, and cholesterol.
    b. Fats, proteins, alcohol, and carbohydrates.
    c. Proteins, fats, carbohydrates, and vitamins and minerals.
    d. Proteins, fats, carbohydrates, and cholesterol.

2. How much of a person's daily calories should come from carbohydrates, according to USDA recommendations?
    a. 55 to 60 percent.
    b. less than 30 percent.
    c. 12 to 15 percent.
    d. less than 10 percent.

3. How much of a person's daily calories should come from protein, according to USDA recommendations?
    a. 55 to 60 percent.
    b. less than 30 percent.
    c. 12 to 15 percent.
    d. less than 10 percent.

4. How much of a person's daily calories should come from fats, according to USDA recommendations?
    a. 55 to 60 percent.
    b. less than 30 percent.
    c. 12 to 15 percent.
    d. less than10 percent.

5. Fiber is a form of carbohydrate that is
    a. not digestible and non-nutritious.
    b. digestible but non-nutritious.
    c. simple and quickly broken down into glucose.
    d. a byproduct of plant development that is not essential to a healthy diet.

Fill in the Blank

1. _____are the measure of how much energy or heat it takes to raise the temperature of 1 kilogram of water by 1 degree Celsius.

2. Although food consists of many components, calories only come from four sources: _____ containing _____ calories per gram, _____ containing _____ calories per gram, _____ containing _____ calories per gram, and _____ containing _____ calories per gram.

3. Simple carbohydrates, such as _____ or table sugar, _____ or fruit sugar, _____ or the sugar found in milk, are quickly broken down into _____ and absorbed by the body.

4. Carbohydrates are composed of sugars and are classified as _____ or _____.

5. The sensation of fullness in the body provided by fats is known as _____.

Matching

_____ 1. fat-soluble

_____ 2. vegan

_____ 3. emulsify

_____ 4. caramelization

_____ 5. noncaloric nutrients

_____ 6. kilocalories

a. water, vitamins, and minerals

b. diet excluding all animal products or byproducts

c. measure of energy

d. to combine two substances that do not normally mix

e. browning of starch or sugar caused by exposure to heat

f. stored in fat tissue

Written/Short Answer

1. Briefly explain the four sources of calories in food, their nutritional function, and the recommended intake of each one.

_____

_____

_____

_____

2. List the food groups in the USDA Food Guide Pyramid and the suggested daily servings for each group.

_____

_____

_____

_____

3. What are the nutritional functions of the two types of fiber? Name some sources of each type.

_____

_____

_____

_____

4. What are the culinary functions of fat?

_____

_____

_____

_____

5. What are the three types of fats and how do they differ?

_____

_____

_____

_____

CHAPTER 4

FOOD AND KITCHEN SAFETY

Chapter Overview

The importance of food and kitchen safety cannot be overemphasized. Few things are as detrimental to a foodservice establishment as an officially noted outbreak of a food-borne illness caused by poor sanitary practices. In addition to providing a sanitary atmosphere and adhering to procedures for safe food handling, it is also important to ensure a safe working environment. This chapter covers the causes of food-borne illnesses and prevention procedures and also includes checklists to help the staff achieve sanitary and safe kitchen conditions.

Chapter Objectives

After reading and studying this chapter, you will be able to:

➤ explain what is meant by adulterated foods and the ways in which foods become adulterated

➤ name the types of pathogens responsible for food-borne illness, and describe how they affect foods as well as how they reproduce in foods

➤ name and explain the three conditions for pathogen growth in foods (potentially hazardous foods)

➤ list and use several techniques to avoid cross contamination

➤ explain the importance of proper hand washing

➤ keep foods out of the danger zone

➤ hold, cool, reheat, and serve cooked or ready-to-serve foods safely

➤ thawing frozen foods safely

➤ explain what is meant by Hazard Analysis Critical Control Points (HACCP) and describe the use of a HACCP plan in a professional kitchen

➤ maintain a properly safe kitchen and dining room environment through proper cleaning, sanitizing, and pest control

➤ explain what is meant by kitchen safety and list several guidelines and techniques for maintaining safety in the kitchen and dining room

➤ identify the appropriate regulations, inspections, and certifications required of foodservice personnel

Study Outline

Food-borne Illness

Chart: Food-borne Illnesses

Key Terms and Concepts

adulterated foods
Aw scale
bacteria
bacteria growth and
    reproduction
biological contaminants

endospores
food-borne illness
infection
intoxication
microorganism
parasites

pathogens
pH level/scale
potentially hazardous foods
viruses

Adulterated Foods

Key Terms and Concepts

chemical contaminants
physical contaminants

biological contaminants
intoxication

infection

Pathogens Responsible For Food-Borne Illness

fungi
    molds
    yeast
viruses
parasites
bacteria
    aerobic
    anaerobic
    facultative
    sensitivity of temperature
    reproduction by fission
    formation of endospores

    three conditions for growth
        (potentially hazardous foods)
    protein source
    water activity (Aw)
    moderate pH

Avoiding Cross Contamination

Key Terms and Concepts

Cross contamination
double strength sanitizing solution
personal hygiene

single-use food-handling gloves
unsanitary handling procedures

Proper Hand Washing

Keeping Foods out of the Danger Zone

Key Terms and Concepts

danger zone
dry storage
expiration date
FIFO/first in, first out

41 to 140°F/5 to 60°C
reach-in refrigerator
sanitary conditions

time and temperature controls
unsanitary conditions
walk-in refrigerator

Receive And Store Foods Safely
Hold Cooked or Ready-to-Serve Foods Safely

Key Terms and Concepts

cold-holding equipment
hot-holding equipment
hot foods hot, cold foods cold

Cooling Foods Safely

Key Terms and Concepts

cooling foods
ice water bath
two-stage cooling method

Reheating Foods Safely

Key Terms and Concepts

food handler
instant-read thermometer
reheat

Thawing Frozen Foods Safely

Key Terms and Concepts

frozen foods
thaw
microwave

Serving Foods Safely

Cleaning and Sanitizing

Key Terms and Concepts

chemical agent/sanitizer
clean/cleaning
double-strength sanitizing

solution
sanitize/sanitizing
three-compartment sink

ware-washing machine

Kitchen Safety

Key Terms and Concepts

fundamentals of good
   personal hygiene
CPR
first aid
mouth-to-mouth resuscitation
Heimlich maneuver
comprehensive fire safety
   plan
employee training
equipment up to code

fire code
fire control system (Ansul
   system)
fire department phone
   number
fire drill
fire
   extinguisher/maintenance
   and inspection of
apron

neckerchief
potentially dangerous
   environment
sanitary uniform
side towel
toque or hat

Health and Hygiene
Working Safely
Fire Safety
Dressing for Safety

Regulations, Inspection, and Certification

Key Terms and Concepts

Americans with Disabilities Act (ADA)
Health and Human Services Administration
Occupational Safety and Health Administration
   (OSHA)
on-site inspection

reporting violations
safe and healthy work environment
a special note about smokers
drugs and alcohol in the workplace

Chapter 4 Exercises

True/False

Indicate whether each of the following statements is True (T) or False (F)

1. Using the FIFO system is essential for food items stored under refrigeration. It does not apply to dry storage areas.

2. Thawing frozen foods under refrigeration is the best but slowest thawing method available.

3. Using the two-stage cooling method endorsed by the FDA, foods are cooled down to a safe temperature in a total of six hours.

4. The proper and quickest way to cool hot liquids is to place them in a plastic container or bowl and set that container in an ice water bath.

5. Foods should never be cooked or reheated in hot-holding equipment because they may stay in the danger zone longer than is considered safe.

6. One of the leading causes of food-borne illness is improperly cooled foods.

7. Foods left in the danger zone for more than two cumulative hours are considered dangerous.

8. Once food has been left in the danger zone longer than is considered safe, the only way to "recover" the food or make it safe is to freeze it.

9. Intoxicating pathogens are destroyed during cooking, so there is little danger of food-borne illness once a food is cooked and held above the danger zone.

10. When computing the amount of time food has spent in the danger zone, the time is cumulative, meaning you must count every time the food enters the danger zone.

Multiple Choice

1. Certain bacteria are able to form endospores, which allow the bacteria to
    a. resume its life cycle if favorable conditions reoccur.
    b. grow in a moist atmosphere.
    c. reproduce every twenty minutes or so.
    d. reproduce outside of the normal pH range.

2. Food is at its greatest risk of cross contamination
   a. during its preparation stage.
   b. during the cooking stage.
   c. when it is being plated with other food.
   d. during holding and storage.

3. When reheating foods, one of the safest methods is to use
   a. steam table.
   b. bain-marie.
   c. chafing dish.
   d. flattop.

4. The pH level most suited for bacterial growth is
   a. 0.85
   b. between 2 and 4
   c. between 5 and 10.
   d. between 12 and 14.

5. The danger zone is generally considered to be
   a. below 41°F/5°C.
   b. between 41 and 100°F/5 and 38°C.
   b. between 41 and 140°F/5 and 60°C.
   c. between 100 and 140°F/38 and 60°C.

Fill in the Blank

1. _____ occurs when disease-causing elements or harmful substances are transferred from one contaminated surface to another.

2. The _____ refers to the temperature range that provides the most suitable environment for pathogens to grow and reproduce.

3. The double-breasted design of the chef's jacket serves two purposes, to _____ and _____.

4. Four important features a restaurant should have to prevent fires and respond to fires should they occur, include _____, _____, _____, and _____. (Could also include fire control systems, fire department phone numbers, properly inspected equipment which is up to code.)

5. _____ refers to the removal of soil or food particles, whereas (sanitizing) involves using moist heat or chemical agents to kill pathogenic microorganisms.

Matching

_____ 1. pathogen

_____ 2. pH

_____ 3. sanitize

_____ 4. FIFO

_____ 5. OSHA

_____ 6. cross contamination

a. agency that ensures a safe and healthy work environment

b. method or storing goods

c. disease causing bacteria

d. measure of acidity or alkalinity

e. using moist heat or chemical agents to kill pathogenic microorganisms

f. transfer of disease causing elements from one item to another

Written/Short Answers

1. Discuss elements of a fire safety plan in a food service establishment.

_____

_____

_____

_____

2. What are some things that can be done to prevent pest infestation?

_____

_____

_____

_____

3. Briefly discuss what can be done to prevent food-borne illness.

_____

_____

_____

_____

4. Briefly discuss how to avoid cross contamination?

_____

_____

_____

_____

5.   What is the danger zone?

_____

_____

_____

_____

CHAPTER **5**

EQUIPMENT IDENTIFICATION

Chapter Overview

Tools, large and small, are what make it possible for a chef to do the job well, and using the right tool for the job is one of the hallmarks of a professional. Equally important is the ability to handle and care for all tools, whether it be a cutting board, a knife, a mandoline, or a stockpot. Professional trade shows and journals allow culinarians to keep up with the latest equipment innovations and learn time- and labor-saving tricks and techniques.

Chapter Objectives

After reading and studying this chapter, you will be able to:

➢ use the rules for knife care, use and storage to perform all cutting tasks safely and efficiently

➢ identify the basic parts of a knive

➢ identify a variety of knives and use them properly

➢ list a number of sharpening and honing tools and explain how to use sharpening and honing technqiues to keep knives functioning safely and efficiently

➢ name a variety of hand tools, describe their function, select and use these tools properly to complete a specific task

➢ name a variety of small equipment, including measuring equipment, sieves and strainers,

➢ name the characteristics of the materials used to manufacture pots, pans, and molds and list the correct procedures for using and cleanings them

➢ identify large equipment used to grind, slice, mix, puree foods

➢ list the guidelines for working safely with large equipment

➢ name and describe a variety of ranges and ovens and their appropriate use

➢ name and describe various types of refrigeration equipment

Study Outline

Knives

Key Terms and Concepts

Arkansas stone
blade
bolster
boning knife
carbon steel blade
carborundum stone
chef's knife
cleaver
cutting edge
diamond-impregnated stone
electric sharpener
filleting knife
flexible-bladed knife
French knife

full tang
grinding wheel
grit
handle
heel
high-carbon stainless steel
    blade
hollow-ground blade
hone
knife kit
knife roll
leather strop
paring knife
partial tang

rat-tail tang
rivets
serrated knife
sharpening stone
slicer
spine
stainless steel blade
steel
tang
taper-ground blade
tip
tourné knife
utility knife

Guidelines for Knives

1. Handle knives with respect.
2. Keep knives sharp.
3. Keep knives clean.
4. Use safe handling procedures for knives.
5. Use an appropriate cutting surface.
6. Keep knives properly stored.

Parts of a knife

Blades
Carbon steel
Stainless steel
High-carbon stainless steel

Taper-ground
Hollow-ground
Tangs
Handles

Rivets
Bolsters

Types of knives

Chef's knife, or French knife
Utility knife
Paring knife

Boning knife
Filleting knife
Slicer

Cleaver
Tourné knife

Sharpening and honing

Sharpening stones
Carborundum stones
Arkansas stones
Diamond-impregnated stones

Guidelines for sharpening knives on a stone

1. Allow yourself enough room to work.
2. Anchor the stone to keep it from slipping as you work.
3. Lubricate the stone with mineral oil or water.
4. Begin sharpening the edge on the coarsest grit you require.
5. Run the entire edge over the surface of the stone, keeping the pressure on the knife even.
6. Always sharpen the blade in the same direction.
7. Make strokes of equal number and equal pressure on each side of the blade.
8. Finish sharpening on the finest stone, and wash and dry the knife thoroughly before use or storage.

Steels

Guidelines for honing knives on a steel

1. Allow yourself plenty of room as you work, and stand with your weight evenly distributed.
2. Draw the blade along the steel so that the entire edge touches the steel.
3. Be sure to keep the pressure even to avoid wearing away the metal in the center of the edge.
4. Use a light touch, stroking evenly and consistently.
5. Repeat the stroke on the opposite side of the edge to properly straighten the edge.

Sharpening Method One

Sharpening Method Two

Steeling Method One

Steeling Method Two

Hand Tools

Key Terms and Concepts

balloon whip
cherry pitter
cutting board
French-style pin
kitchen fork
ladle
melon baller
metal spatula
offset spatula

palette knife metal spatula
Parisienne scoop melon
baller
pastry bag
rod-and-bearing pin
rolling pin
rotary peeler
rubber scraper
sauce whip

scoop
skimmer
spider
spoon
strawberry huller
swivel-bladed peeler
tomato knife
whip/whisk

Small Equipment

Key Terms and Concepts

balance beam scale
bouillon strainer
mixing bowl
candy thermometer
champignon
cheesecloth
chinois
colander

conical sieve
deep-fat thermometer
drum sieve
electronic scale
food mill
french-fry cutter
garlic press
graduated measuring pitcher

instant-read thermometer
measuring spoon
ricer
spring-type scale
storage container
strainer
tamis

Measuring Equipment

Graduated measuring pitchers
Scales

Thermometers
Measuring spoons

Sieves and Strainers

Food mill
Drum sieve (tamis)
Conical sieve (chinois)

Colander
Ricer
Cheesecloth

Bowls for Mixing

Storage Containers

Pots, Pans, and Molds

Key Terms and Concepts

bain-marie
brasier
cake pan
chafing dish
couscousière
crêpe pan
dariole mold
double boiler
fait-tout
fish poacher
gauge
gratin dish
griddle
grill pan
griswold
hotel pan

kugelhopf form
loaf pan
loose-bottom tart pan/tartlet
pan
marmite
muffin tin
omelet pan
paella pan
pâté mold
pie pan
ring mold
roasting pan
rondeau
sauce pan
sauce pot
sauté pan

sauteuse
sautoir
savarin mold
sheet pan
skillet
soufflé dish
springform pan
steamer
stockpot
terrine mold
tiered steamer
timbale mold
tube pan
wok

Guidelines for selecting pots and pans

1. Choose a size appropriate to the food being cooked.
2. Choose material appropriate to the cooking technique.
3. Use proper handling, cleaning, and storing techniques.

Pots and Pans for Stovetop Cooking

Stockpot (marmite)
Sauce pot
Saucepan
Rondeau

Sauteuse
Sautoir
Omelet pan/crêpe pan
Bain-marie (double boiler)

Griddle
Fish poacher
Steamer
Specialty pots and pans

Pans for Oven Cooking

Roasting pan
Sheet pan
Hotel pans
Pâté mold
Terrine mold
Gratin dish

Soufflé dish
Timbale mold
Specialty molds
Cake pans
Springform pans
Loose-bottom tart pans

Pie pans
Loaf pans
Muffin tins
Tube pans
Kugelhopf forms

Large Equipment

Key Terms and Concepts

blender
broiler
buffalo chopper
burr mixer
combi oven
convection oven
convection steamer
conventional oven
conveyor oven
deck oven
deep-fat fryer
display refrigeration
flattop range
food chopper
food processor

food/meat slicer
griddle
grill
hand blender
immersion blender
induction cooktop
mandoline
meat grinder
microwave oven
on-site refrigeration
open-burner range
pizza oven
portable refrigeration
pressure steamer
reach-in refrigerator

ring-top range
rotary oven
rotating deck oven
salamander
smoker
standing mixer
steam-jacketed kettle
stick blender
Swiss brasier
tilting frying pan
tilting kettle
tilting skillet
vertical chopping machine
(VCM)
walk-in refrigerator

Guidelines for using large equipment

1. Obtain proper instructions in the machine's safe operation.
2. First turn off and then unplug electrical equipment before assembling it or breaking it down.
3. Use all safety features: Be sure that lids are secure, hand guards are used, and the machine is stable.
4. Clean and sanitize the equipment thoroughly after each use.
5. Be sure that all pieces of equipment are properly reassembled and left unplugged after each use.
6. Report any problems or malfunctions promptly, and alert coworkers to the problem.

Grinding, Slicing, Mixing, and Puréeing Equipment

Meat grinder
Blender
Food processor
Immersion blender

Vertical chopping machine
(VCM)
Food chopper (buffalo
chopper)

Food/meat slicer
Mandoline
Standing mixer

Kettles and Steamers

Steam-jacketed kettle
Tilting kettle

Pressure steamer
Convection steamer

Deep-fat fryer

Ranges and Ovens

Ovens
Open-burner range
Flattop range
Ring-top range

Induction cooktop
Convection oven
Conventional/deck ovens
Combi oven

Microwave oven
Other styles

Griddles and Grills

Griddle
Grill/broiler/salamander

Smokers

Refrigeration Equipment

Walk-in
Reach-in

On-site refrigeration
Portable refrigeration

Display refrigeration

Professional Chefs and Their Tools

Chapter 5 Exercises

True/False

Indicate whether each of the following statements is True (T) or False (F)

_____ 1. A steel should be used both before and after sharpening a blade on a sharpening stone.

_____ 2. Anodized aluminum and stainless steel are the preferred materials for stockpots.

_____ 3. Stainless steel knife blades must be treated carefully to avoid discoloration, rusting, and pitting.

_____ 4. Copper pots are often cleaned with a homemade solution of flour, salt, and white vinegar.

_____ 5. Cast-iron pans are seasoned by applying oil to the surface and then placing them in a 400°F/205°C oven for one hour.

_____ 6. Taper-ground knife blades have been forged out of a single sheet of metal and have more longevity than hollow-ground blades.

_____ 7. A rat-tail tang is preferable over a partial tang because it is not visible at the top or bottom edge.

_____ 8. A filleting knife is used to cut meat and chicken into fillets.

_____ 9. A bolster is the sheath or wrap used to carry a chef's knife, often worn on the belt.

_____ 10. A lubricant is used when sharpening knives on a stone to reduce the friction.

Multiple Choice

1. Because it will take and keep a sharp edge without discoloring or rusting, the most frequently used material for knife blades today is
   a. carbon steel.
   b. stainless steel.
   c. high-carbon stainless steel.
   d. aluminum.

2. The knife best suited for all-purpose chopping, slicing, and mincing is the
   a. chef's knife.
   b. utility knife.
   c. slicer.
   d. cleaver.

3. The large knife often used for chopping and cutting through bones is the
   a. chef's knife.
   b. utility knife.
   c. boning knife.
   d. cleaver.

4. Grit refers to
   a. the shavings that come off the knife during sharpening.
   b. the coarseness or fineness of a sharpening stone's surface.
   c. the coarseness or fineness of a sharpening steel.
   d. the wheel used to hold a sharpening stone.

5. Copper mixing bowls are often included in the kitchen's stock of mixing bowls because
   a. they are best for whipping certain items.
   b. they are more durable.
   c. they are safer.
   d. they look more attractive when presented to the guests.

Fill in the Blank

1. Copper mixing bowls are often included in the kitchen's stock of mixing bowls because

   _____.

2. A combi oven is a combination _____ and _____.

3. To purée foods directly in the cooking vessels they have been prepared in, you should use a__

   _____.

4. When food needs to be cooked or heated very gently on the stovetop, the best pot would be a

   _____.

5. The tool best suited to turn or lift foods on grills, broilers, and griddles is the _____
   _____. _____is a round-tipped tool is used for turning pancakes and
   grilled foods and is also used in the bakeshop to apply icings and fillings.

Matching

_____ 1. burr mixer   _____ 4. chinois

_____ 2. spider   _____ 5. steel

_____ 3. bolster   _____ 6. tilting kettle

a. tool used to lift food out of liquid or fat
b. tool used to hone knives
c. immersion blender
d. conical sieve
e. large, freestanding unit for braising, sautéing, and steaming
f. collar or shank of a knife

Written/Short Answer

1. What are the parts of a knife? Give the ideal specifications for each part.

   _____

   _____

   _____

   _____

2. What are the general guidelines for working with sharpening stones?

   _____

_____

_____

_____

3.   What are the general guidelines for honing a knife with a steel?

_____

_____

_____

_____

4.   What guidelines should be observed for selecting a pot, pan, or mold?

_____

_____

_____

_____

5.   What are some guidelines to follow when using large equipment and electrical appliances?

_____

_____

_____

_____

CHAPTER **6**

Meat, Poultry, and Game Identification

Chapter Overview

For most restaurants, the purchase, preparation, and service of meats is one of the most expensive areas of the business—but also one of the most potentially profitable. In order to get the most value out of the meats purchased, it is important to understand how to select the right cut for a particular cooking method.

Chapter Objectives

After reading and studying this chapter, you will be able to

➢ explain such basic meat concepts as inspection, grading, and storage of beef, veal, pork, lamb, venison, and poultry

➢ explain the difference between meat inspection and quality grading

➢ identify a variety of cuts for each type of meat and game

➢ identify a variety of types of poultry and game birds

➢ pair specific cuts of meat or poultry with the appropriate cooking method(s)

Study Outline

Meat Basics

Key Terms and Concepts

antemortem	grading	select
butcher's paper	inspection stamp	shohet
choice	kosher meats	United States Department Of
Cryovac	*The Meat Buyer's Guide*	Agriculture (USDA)
cutability	National Association of Meat	USDA grade shield
fabrication	Purveyors (NAMP)	wholesome
freshness	postmortem	yield grade
government inspection	prime	

Market Forms of Meat

Key Terms and Concepts

boxed meat
butchering
fabrication
hanging meat

primal cut
quarter
retail cut
saddle

side
subprimal

Beef

Key Terms and Concepts

"higher" flavor
aged beef
bone-in
boneless
bottom round
Brae beef
brisket
Certified Angus beef
châteaubriand
chuck
corned brisket/corned beef
double cut
English cut
fillet mignon
flank
foreshank

fresh brisket
ground meat
heart
hindshank
honeycomb tripe
king cut
Kobe beef
Limousin beef
liver
loin
medallion
miscellaneous cuts of beef
natural beef
New York strip
organic beef
oxtail

prime rib
queen's cut
rib
roast
round
shank
shoulder
skirt steak
steak
strip loin
tenderloin
tenderloin tips
tongue
top round
tournedos
tripe

Veal

Key Terms and Concepts

bone-in
boneless
bones
brains
breast
chops
chuck
cutlet
escalopes
feet
fore quarter
foresaddle
foreshank
Frenched

ground meat
head
heart
hind quarter
hind shank
hindsaddle
leg
liver
loin
medallions
milk-fed veal
nature-fed veal
offal
organ meats

paillard
rack
rib
roast
scallop
scaloppini
shank
shoulder
sweetbreads
tongue
top round
variety meats

Pork

Key Terms and Concepts

baby back ribs
bacon
bone-in
boneless
Boston butt
butt
chops
chops
clear fat
country-style ribs
crown roast
cured

cutlets
daisy ham
fatback
ground pork
ham
ham hocks
knuckles
leg
loin
medallions
noisettes
picnic butt

picnic ham
pig's feet
rib chops
roasts
shoulder
sirloin chops
slab bacon
smoked
snouts
spareribs
streak of lean
tenderloin

Lamb and Mutton

Key Terms and Concepts

breast
foresaddle
hindsaddle
hothouse lamb

leg
loin
mutton
rack

rib
shank
shoulder
spring lamb

Venison and Other Furred Game

Key Terms and Concepts

bear
elk
fallow deer
farm-raised deer
game meat

haunch
leg
loin
rabbit
rib

shank
shoulder
venison
wild boar

Domestic

Key Terms and Concepts

back
boneless breast
breast
breast with neck and back
   attached
broiler
chicken
chicken feet
cock's combs
Cornish game hen
cutlets
duckling
foie gras
fowl
free-range
fryer
game birds
geese and ducks
gizzard

gosling
heart
leg
livers
Long Island duck
mature hen (turkey)
mature tom (turkey)
moulard duck
Muscovy duck
natural
neck
organic
parts
Pekin duck
pheasant
poultry
poussins
quail
rendered chicken fat

roaster
Rock Cornish hen
scallops
schmaltz
snipe
squab
stewing hen
teal
thigh
turkey
USDA grades (A, B, C)
whole bird
wild duck
wild turkey
young hen (turkey)
young tom (turkey)

Chapter 6 Exercises

True/False

Indicate whether each of the following statements is True (T) or False (F)

_____ 1. Rock Cornish hens are highly valued because the ratio of dark meat to light meat is greater than in other birds.

_____ 2. Beef steaks cut from the rib are always bone-in, steaks cut from the loin are boneless.

3. Some cuts from the beef round are suitable for roasting and may be used successfully for some roasted menu items.

_____ 4. The key to preparing and serving tender flank and skirt steaks is to not overcook them and to cut them correctly.

_____ 5. Because beef liver has a deeper color and more pronounced flavor than veal liver, it is more popular on menus.

_____ 6.   Veal bones and feet are excellent for preparing stock and foundation sauces.

_____ 7.   The term "ham" refers to pork leg that has been cured or smoked.

_____ 8.   Medallions or noisettes can be prepared successfully from pork, beef, or veal tenderloin.

_____ 9.   Pork spareribs are similar cuts to beef short ribs, breast of veal, and breast of lamb.

_____ 10. Fallow deer produces a lean, tasty meat with less fat and cholesterol than beef.

Multiple Choice

1. Veal cutlets or scaloppini are best when fabricated from the
   a. chuck/shoulder.
   b. rib.
   c. loin.
   d. round.

2. Fillet mignon is fabricated from the
   a. chuck/shoulder.
   b. rib.
   c. loin.
   d. round.

3. Pork medallions are fabricated from the
   a. shoulder.
   b. sparerib.
   c. loin.
   d. leg.

4. When preparing a grilled beef steak, one of the better cuts to choose from would be
   a. chuck.
   b. rib.
   c. round.
   d. shank.

5. When preparing beef stew, the cut that would be most economical and satisfactory would be:
   a. top round.
   b. tenderloin tips.
   c. skirt steak.
   d. rib.

Fill in the Blank

1. In the process of aging beef and other meats, there is an increase of _____ and a decrease of _____.

2. The chef should separate different kinds of meat in the refrigeration unit in order to _____ _____.

3. Once meat is unwrapped or removed from Cryovac, it should be rewrapped in _____ _____to reduce spoilage or contamination.

4. Once an animal carcass is cut into four pieces, it is cut further into what are referred to as _____, and then further broken down into _____. If those cuts are fabricated into steaks, chops, roasts, ground meat, or other items, they are referred to as _____.

5. The *clear fat* that runs along the pig's back is known as _____. The *streak of lean* is known as _____.

Matching

_____ 1. Cryovac

_____ 2. picnic ham

_____ 3. corned beef

_____ 4. schmaltz

_____ 5. cutability

_____ 6. foie gras

a. rendered chicken fat

b. a special type of plastic wrapping

c. fattened liver of the moulard duck

d. measure of yield of meat

e. cured and brined brisket

f. cut from shoulder of pork

Written/Short Answer

1. How should meat be stored and for how long?

_____

_____

_____

_____

2. Briefly explain the significance to the chef of the federal requirements for inspection, grading, and yield grades.

_____

_____

_____

_____

3. What are variety meats?

_____

_____

_____

_____

4. Explain the statement that you can use everything on the pig except the oink.

_____

_____

_____

_____

5. Discuss the cooking techniques used for venison and other furred game.

_____

_____

_____

_____

6. What are the market forms of meat?

_____

_____

_____

_____

7. How is chicken graded and classified and what cooking methods generally apply?

_____

_____

_____

_____

Essay

1. What factors should the chef consider when deciding what type/cut/style of meat to buy?

2. What should the chef check for/look at when receiving/accepting meat that has been ordered?

CHAPTER 7

FISH AND SHELLFISH IDENTIFICATION

Chapter Overview

Fish were once plentiful and inexpensive, but because of various factors, including increased popularity, pollution of fishing beds, and the search for variety, demand has begun to outstrip supply. Also, many countries have passed regulations limiting commercial fishing in specific waters.

What this means to most chefs and consumers is that many longtime menu favorites, including bluefish, true striped bass, and red snapper, are increasingly unavailable. However, aquaculture, or farm-raising of fish, is growing, and it is becoming one of the few reliable sources of fresh fish. Today, farm-raised hybrid striped bass, trout, salmon, tilapia, catfish, oysters, mussels, and clams are easily found.

Chapter Objectives

After reading and studying this chapter, you will be able to:

➤ name the basic market forms for flat and round fish and shellfish

➤ identify a number of fish and categorize them (flat or round, lean or oily)

➤ pair specific fish with the appropriate cooking method(s)

➤ handle fish and shellfish safely during storage and preparation

➤ name the basic guidelines for purchasing fish and shellfish

➤ identify a number of shellfish and categorize them (mollusk, crustacean, cephalopod)

➤ pair specific shellfish with the appropriate cooking method(s)

Study Outline

Fish Basics

Key Terms and Concepts

drawn	flat fish	round fish
dressed	liquor	salted
fabrication/fabricating	mollusk	scales/scaling
fillet	pan-dressed	shell
fins	pickled	shucked
fishmonger	purveyor	smoked

steak   viscera   whole

Market Forms

Whole fish   Dressed fish   Fillets
Drawn fish   Steaks   Shucked

Storing and handling fish

1. Check the fish carefully for freshness and quality.
2. Place the fish on a bed of shaved or flaked ice in a perforated container; stainless steel or plastic is preferred.
3. Cover with additional ice; the fish may be layered, if necessary with shaved or flaked ice.
4. Set the perforated container inside a second container.
5. Re-ice fish daily.

Commonly Available Fish

Key Terms and Concepts

albacore tuna	farm-raised	monkfish
anchovy	fatty	mutton snapper
anchovy paste	Finnan haddie	nonbony fish
angler fish	flatfish	oily fish
Atlantic cod	flounder	perch
Atlantic salmon	goosefish	pike
baccala	gravad lox	pike
bass	gray snapper	pink snapper
beeliner snapper	gray sole	plaice
belly fish	grouper	planking
black sea bass	haddock	pollock
blacktip shark	hake	pompano
blue shark	halibut	rainbow trout
bluefish	hybrid striped bass	ray
brown trout	king mackerel	red grouper
catfish	king salmon	red snapper
cod	lawyer fish	red snapper
coho salmon	lemon sole	roughback
croaker	lotte	round fish
cusk	mackerel	salmon
dolphin fish	mahi mahi	salmon trout
Dover sole	mako shark	salt cod
drum	mangrove snapper	sand dab
eel	mollusks	sea bass

sea bream
sea trout
shad
shad roe
shark
silk snapper
skate
skate wings
smoked trout

snapper
Spanish mackerel
squeteaque
steelhead trout
striped bass
swordfish
trout
tuna
turbot

vermilion snapper
walleyed pike
weakfish
white sole
whiting
yellowtail snapper
yellowtip shark

Key Terms and Concepts

Anchovy
Bass
Bluefish
Catfish
Cod
Dover sole
Dolphin fish (Mahi mahi)
Eel
Flounder

Grouper
Halibut
Mackerel
Monkfish
Perch
Pike
Pompano
Salmon
Shad

Shark
Skate, Ray
Snapper
Swordfish
Trout
Tuna
Turbot
Weakfish

Shellfish

Key Terms and Concepts

abalone
American lobster
bay scallop
blue crab
blue crab
calico scallop
cherrystone clams
clams
conch
count
crab
crawfish
crayfish
debeard
Dublin Bay prawn
Dungeness crab
escargot

flash-freeze
freshwater
gastropod
tomalley
hard-shell clams
head off
head on
ink
Jonah crab
king crab
littleneck clam
lobster
lobster roe
lobster tail
lobsterette
Maine lobster
mussels

octopus
oysters
quahog
rock lobster
saltwater
scallop
sea scallop
shrimp
shucked
snails
soft-shell clam
soft-shell crab
spider crab
spiny lobster
squid
stone crab
whelk

General categories for shellfish

Univalves (single-shelled mollusks)
Bivalves (with two shells joined by a hinge)
Crustaceans (with jointed exterior skeletons or shells)
Cephalopods

Abalone	Mussels	Shrimp
Conch	Oysters	Octopus
Snails	Scallops	Squid
Clams	Crab	Shrimp chart
Hard-shell clam or quahog	Crayfish	
Soft-shell clams	Lobster	

Chapter 7 Exercises

True/False

Indicate whether each of the following statements is True (T) or False (F)

_____ 1. When purchasing mackerel, king mackerel is considered to be superior to Spanish mackerel.

_____ 2. When determining cooking method for any fish you should consider the fat content and texture of the fish.

_____ 3. With few exceptions, all trout sold in the Unites States comes from commercial hatcheries.

_____ 4. Other than for the ubiquitous tuna salad, fresh tuna is always preferred over canned tuna in restaurant cooking.

_____ 5. When purchasing fish, if the skin feels slick and moist, it indicates that the enzymes are beginning to deteriorate and the fish is not fresh.

_____ 6. When purchasing fish, the gills should be a good red to maroon color, with no traces of gray or brown.

_____ 7. Dolphin fish, although technically a mammal, is considered a fish for culinary purposes because it shares many of the same characteristics as round fish.

_____ 8. Anchovies are always sold canned or as paste because laws prohibit them being transported live.

_____ 9. Saltwater species of bass are harvested in both the Atlantic and Pacific.

_____ 10. Frozen and canned abalone is the most common form of abalone available because California state law prohibits the exportation of live abalone.

Multiple Choice

1. Clams, mussels, and oysters purchased live should be
   a. stored on ice.
   b. frozen and held at -10°F/-23°C
   c. held at 35 to 40°F/1 to 4°C
   d. cooked immediately and held at held at 35 to 40°F/1 to 4°C

2. Bluefish is best prepared by using
   a. any/all cooking methods.
   b. grilling or broiling.
   c. poaching or steaming.
   d. deep frying.

3. Black sea bass is best prepared by using
   a. any/all cooking methods.
   b. grilling or broiling.
   c. moist-heat cooking techniques.
   d. dry-heat cooking techniques.

4. Mackerel is best suited for
   a. any/all cooking methods.
   b. combination cooking techniques.
   c. moist-heat cooking techniques.
   d. dry-heat cooking techniques.

5. Shark is commonly prepared using
   a. any/all cooking methods.
   b. combination cooking techniques.
   c. moist-heat cooking techniques.
   d. dry-heat cooking techniques.

Fill in the Blank

1. The less expensive shark is sometimes sold to the unwary as swordfish. Swordfish's darker strip of flesh has _____pattern, which is one way to distinguish it from shark, which has a _____pattern.

2. Two kinds of hard-shelled clams are _____ and _____.
   Anything larger than 3 inches in diameter is referred to as a _____.

3. Lemon sole and gray sole are common market names for types of _____.

4. Dolphin fish is commonly marketed as _____.

5. Five round fish that are commonly cut into steaks and can be broiled or grilled are

   _____, _____, _____, _____,

   and _____. Note: could also include bluefish, grouper, pompano,
   monkfish.

Matching

_____ 1. shucked   _____ 4. drawn

_____ 2. tomalley   _____ 5. roe

_____ 3. viscera   _____ 6. conch

a. fish with guts removed, but head and tail intact
b. lobster liver
c. gastropod found in the Caribbean
d. fish guts
e. fish or mollusk removed from shell
f. fish eggs

Written/Short Answer

1. What are the four categories of shellfish based on their skeletal structures? Name two
   examples of each.

   _____

   _____

   _____

   _____

2. What are some things to look for when purchasing/receiving fish?

   _____

   _____

   _____

   _____

3. What are the guidelines for storing fish?

_____

_____

_____

_____

4. Name and explain the 3 categories of fish based on their skeletal structure. Give 2 examples of each.

_____

_____

_____

_____

5. What do you look for when purchasing live shellfish?

_____

_____

_____

_____

6. How should you store live shellfish?

_____

_____

_____

_____

7. What are the market forms of commercially available fish?

_____

_____

_____

_____

Essay

1. What are some things a chef should watch out for/be wary of when purchasing/receiving fish?

2. How do you pair a fish with a particular cooking technique? What must you consider when deciding on recipe and menu items?

CHAPTER 8

F RUIT, V EGETABLE, AND F RESH H ERB I DENTIFICATION

Chapter Overview

Fruits, vegetables, and herbs have always been an important part of the human diet, but today consumers are more aware than ever of the important role these foods play in maintaining overall health and fitness. This chapter provides professional chefs with the information they need to take full advantage of the abundance of fresh produce now available, including tips on availability, determination of quality, and proper storage.

Chapter Objectives

After reading and studying this chapter, you will be able to

➢ list the general guidelines for selecting fresh fruits, vegetables, and herbs

➢ explain what is meant by grading and how this information is used by the chef

➢ name the basic procedures for storing fresh produce

➢ identify and name quality factors for a variety of fresh fruits, vegetables, and herbs

➢ name the general categories for fruits and vegetables

Study Outline

General Guidelines

Key Terms and Concepts

boutique farmers	grade/grading	U.S. Department of
commercial purveyors	herbs	Agriculture (USDA)
ethylene gas	hydroponic growing	vegetables
ethylene-producing fruits	mold	
fruits	nutrients	

Fruits

Key Terms and Concepts

apples
apricots
bananas
Bartlett pears
berries
bigarade oranges
Bing cherries
bitter oranges
black Corinth grapes
black friar plums
black grapes
blackberries
blood oranges
blueberries
Bosc pears
boysenberries
cantaloupes
casaba melons
cherries
citrus fruit
climate-controlled cold
storage
clingstone peaches
cloudberries
Comice pears
Concord grapes
cooking plums
crabapples
cranberries
Crenshaw melons
currants
D'anjou pears
damson plums
dates
dessert plums
dewberry
eating out of hand
elderberries

figs
freestone peaches
Fuji apples
full slip
Gala apples
gallia melons
Golden Delicious apples
gooseberries
Granny Smith apples
grapes
greengage plums
greening apples
guava
honeydew melons
IQF (individually quick-
frozen)
Italian plums
Jonathan apples
juice
juice oranges
Key limes
kiwis
lemons
loganberry
mandarins
mangos
McIntosh apples
melons
Meyer lemons
mulberries
muskmelons
Napoleon Red grapes
navel oranges
nectarines
Northern Spy apples
papayas
passion fruit
peaches

pears
perishable
Persian limes
Persian melons
pie plant
pineapples
pink grapefruits
plantains
plums
pomegranates
prune plums
Queen Anne cherries
raspberries
Red Delicious apples
red emperor grapes
red grapefruits
rhubarb
Rome Beauty apples
Santa Rosa plums
Seckel pears
Seville oranges
star fruit
stone fruits
strawberries
tangerines
temple oranges
Thompson seedless grapes
tropical fruits
ugli fruits
Valencia oranges
watermelons
white grapefruits
William pears
Winesap apples
winter melons
zest

Apples

Crabapples
Golden Delicious apples
Granny Smith apples
Greening apples

Jonathan apples
McIntosh apples
Northern Spy apples
Red Delicious apples

Rome Beauty apples
Winesap apples

Berries

Blueberries	Currants	Raspberries
Boysenberries	Elderberries	Strawberries
Cloudberries	Gooseberries	
Cranberries	Mulberries	

Citrus Fruits

Blood oranges	Tangerines	Persian limes
Juice oranges	Temple oranges	Key limes
Mandarins	Ugli fruits	Pink grapefruits
Navel oranges	Meyer lemons	Red grapefruits
Seville oranges	Lemons	White grapefruits

Grapes

Thompson seedless grapes	Black grapes	Black Corinth grapes
Concord grapes	Red emperor grapes	

Melons

Cantaloupes	Gallia melons	Persian melons
Casaba melons	Honeydew melons	Watermelons
Crenshaw melons	Muskmelons	

Pears

Bartlett pears	Comice pears	Seckel pears
Bosc pears	D'anjou pears	William pears

Rhubarb

Stone fruits

Peaches	Nectarines	Plum
Apricots	Cherries	

Tropical Fruits

Vegetables

Key Terms and Concepts

acorn squash	banana potatoes	black salsify
Anaheims	barlotti beans	black truffles
artichoke hearts	bean sprouts	black-eyed peas
arugula	beans	bliss potatoes
asparagus	beefsteak tomatoes	boiling onions
avocados	beet greens	bok choy
baby beets	beets	boletes
baby lettuce mix	Belgian endive	boletus mushrooms
banana chiles	bell peppers	Boston lettuce

brassica varieties
broccoli
broccoli rabe or raab
brown mushroom
Brussels sprouts
burgundy beans
burpless cucumbers
butterhead lettuce
butternut squash
cabbage family
cabbage turnip
cantarello
caribe potatoes
carrots
cauliflower
celeriac
celery
celery cabbage
cèpes, cep
chanterelles
chayote
chef's potato
cherry tomatoes
chiles
chives
cippolini
cloves
collard greens
Colorado chile
cooking greens
corn
corn salad
cranberry beans
cranberry tomatoes
cremini mushrooms
crookneck squash
cucumbers
cultivated mushrooms
cured onion
curly endive
currant tomatoes
daikon radishes
dandelion greens
dried onion
edible flowers
eggplant
elephant garlic
English cucumbers
escarole

fava beans
fennel
fiddlehead ferns
finferlo
fingerling potatoes
flageolets
fungus
fresh legumes
fresh onion
gallinaccio
garden peas
garden peas
garlic
golden beets
gourd
green beans
green cabbage
green onions
Haas avocados
habaneros
haricot verts
heading cabbage
heading lettuce
heirloom potatoes
horse carrots
hubbard squash
Hungarian wax peppers
iceberg lettuce
Idaho potatoes
Irish potatoes
Jalapeños
Japanese eggplant
Jerusalem artichokes
jícama
kale
kirby cucumbers
kohlrabi
lamb's lettuce
leaf lettuce
leeks
lima beans
loose-head cabbage
loose-head lettuce
mâche
Maui onions
mesclun mix
mirliton
morels
morille

mushrooms
mustard greens
new potatoes
oak leaf
oak mushroom
okra
oyster mushrooms
oyster plant
parsnips
pattypan squash
pear tomatoes
pearl onions
peas
petit pois
plum tomatoes
poblanos
pod vegetables
porcini
portobello mushrooms
potatoes
pumpkins
purple eggplant
purple potatoes
purple-topped turnips
radicchio
radishes
ramps
rapini
red beets
red cabbage
red onions
red potatoes
red radishes
Roma tomatoes
Romaine lettuce
Roman mushroom
Romano beans
roots
ruby chard
russet potatoes
rutabagas
salad greens
salsify
salt potatoes
savoy cabbage
scallions
scarlet runners
Scotch bonnets
seed

seedless cucumbers
serranos
shallots
shiitake mushrooms
shoots
slicing cucumbers
snow peas
spaghetti squash
Spanish onions
spinach leaves
spugnole
squash
stalks
standard eggplant
storage cabbage
sugar snap peas
summer squash
summer squash
sunchokes

sweet corn
sweet onions
sweet peppers
sweet potatoes
Swiss chard
tomatillos
tomatoes
toxic
truffles
tubers
turnip greens
turnips
Vidalia onions
Walla Walla onions
watercress
wax beans
white eggplant
white mushrooms
white onions

white potatoes
white salsify
white truffles
white turnips
wild leeks
wild mushrooms
winter cabbage
winter squash
winter squash
wood ear mushrooms
wrapper leaves
yams
Yellow Finn potatoes
yellow onions
yellow slicing tomatoes
yellow squash
yellow turnips
Yukon gold potatoes
zucchini

Avocados

Cabbage family

Broccoli
Broccoli rabe
Brussels sprouts
Bok choy

Celery cabbage
Green cabbage
Red cabbage
Savoy cabbage

Cauliflower
Kohlrabi

Cucumbers, Squashes, and Eggplant

Slicing cucumbers
Kirby cucumbers
English, burpless, or seedless
cucumbers
Pattypan squash
Chayote

Crookneck squash
Yellow squash
Zucchini
Acorn squash
Butternut squash
Hubbard squash

Pumpkins
Spaghetti squash
Purple (or standard) eggplant
Japanese eggplant
White eggplant

Leafy vegetables

Arugula
Belgian endive
Boston (butterhead) lettuce
Curly endive
Escarole
Iceberg lettuce
Leaf lettuce

Oak leaf
Mâche
Radicchio
Romaine lettuce
Watercress
Beet greens
Collard greens

Dandelion greens
Kale
Mustard greens
Spinach leaves
Swiss chard
Turnip greens

Mushrooms

Boletus mushrooms
Chanterelles
Cremini mushrooms

Morels
Oyster mushrooms
Portobello mushrooms

Shiitake mushrooms
Truffles

Onion Family

Boiling onions
Cippolini
Garlic
Leeks
Pearl onions

Ramps
Red onions
Scallions
Shallots
Spanish onions

Sweet onions
Yellow onions
White onions

Peppers

Anaheims
Banana chiles
Habaneros

Scotch bonnets
Jalapeños
Poblanos

Serranos

Pod and seed vegetables

Green beans
Haricot verts
Romano beans
Burgundy beans

Fava beans
Cranberry beans
Barlotti beans
Flageolets

Black-eyed peas
Garden peas
Snow peas
Sugar snap peas

Potatoes

Chef's potato
Red potatoes
Russet or Idaho potatoes
Heirloom potatoes

Yukon gold potatoes
Irish potatoes
Salt potatoes
New potatoes

Bliss potatoes
Sweet potatoes
Yams

Roots and Tubers

Beets
  Baby beets
  Red beets
  Golden beets
Carrots
Celeriac

Jerusalem artichokes
Jícama
Parsnips
Turnips
  Purple-topped turnips
  Rutabagas

Radishes
  Red radishes
  Daikon radishes
Salsify (oyster plant)
  White salsify
  Black salsify

Shoots and Stalks

Tomatoes

Beefsteak tomatoes
Cherry tomatoes

Currant (or cranberry)
  tomatoes
Pear tomatoes

Plum (Roma) tomatoes
Yellow slicing tomatoes
Tomatillos

Herbs

Key Terms and Concepts

aromatic plants
basil
bay leaves
bouquet garni
chervil
cilantro
curly parsley
dill

fines herbes
flat-leaf parsley
herbs
Italian parsley
marjoram
mint
oregano
parsley

purple basil
rosemary leaves
sage
summer savory
tarragon
thyme
watercress
winter savory

Chapter 8 Exercises

True/False

Indicate whether each of the following statements is True (T) or False (F)

_____ 1. Because of the many varieties of chiles, dried and/or smoked chiles are generally sold under the same name as their fresh version, to avoid confusion.

_____ 2. All sweet (bell) peppers start out green, but certain varieties will ripen into rich, vibrant colors.

_____ 3. Snow peas are eaten whole, pod and pea. Sugar snap peas have an inedible pod, which must be removed before eating.

_____ 4. Haricot verts is the French name for green beans.

_____ 5. Mesclun is a special mix of salad greens, not a variety on its own.

_____ 6. Chefs across the country are beginning to use salad greens as cooking greens because of the potent vitamins and minerals they deliver.

_____ 7. All varieties of eggplant can be cooked in the same manner, braising, roasting, grilling, or stewing.

_____ 8. Traditionally, truffles grew underground and were found by specially trained dogs or pigs who sniffed them out; today commercially marketed truffles are farm-raised.

_____ 9. Belgian endive and watercress are both leafy vegetables that are typically eaten raw in salads like lettuces.

_____ 10. Butterhead lettuce and mâche can be eaten raw in salads, or braised as a vegetable.

Multiple Choice

1. As a general rule, which of the following ripe vegetables should not be refrigerated?
   a. Squash
   b. Potatoes
   c. Beans
   d. Chiles

2. As a general rule, which of the following ripe fruit should not be refrigerated?
   a. Bananas
   b. Pineapple
   c. Grapes
   d. Apples

3. Most vegetables should be left intact when being stored and should just be trimmed before being used, with the following exception:
   a. the outer leaves of lettuces should be removed before storing.
   b. the outer leaves of cabbages should be removed before storing
   c. beans should be removed from inedible pods before storing.
   d. the leafy tops of some root vegetables should be removed before storing.

4. Crabapples are best suited for
   a. eating out of hand.
   b. all purposes.
   c. sauces and relishes.
   d. pies.

5. Granny Smith apples are best suited for
   a. eating out of hand.
   b. all purposes.
   c. sauces and relishes.
   d. pies.

Fill in the Blank

1. Walla Walla, Vidalia, and Maui are all varieties of _____.

2. The common name for the morille or spugnole mushroom is _____.

3. The common name for the gallinaccio or cantarello mushroom is _____.

4. The oak mushroom might be better well known as the _____ mushroom.

5. _____truffles, the finest of which come from _____are always cooked. _____ truffles, the finest of which come from _____are often served raw, thinly shaved over risotto or pasta dishes.

Matching

_____ 1. kohlrabi
_____ 2. Northern Spy
_____ 3. chayote
_____ 4. Seville
_____ 5. mâche
_____ 6. Thompson

a. grapes, often dried for raisins

b. bitter orange

c. round, turnip-shaped member of cabbage family

d. crisp, firm apple

e. lamb's lettuce, or corn salad

f. type of squash, also known as mirliton

Written/Short Answer

1. How should fruits and vegetables be stored?

_____

_____

_____

_____

2. What is the concern about ethylene gas from a culinary standpoint?

_____

_____

_____

_____

3. What is hydroponic growing?

_____

_____

_____

_____

4. How are fruits and vegetables graded? Why should the chef have knowledge of grades?

_____

_____

_____

_____

5. How does purchasing and the holding quality of pod and seed vegetables differ from other vegetables?

_____

_____

_____

_____

6. How should fresh herbs be stored?

_____

_____

_____

_____

7. Why are cooking greens becoming popular in contemporary kitchens?

_____

_____

_____

_____

Essay

1. Briefly discuss the selection and use of fresh herbs in the contemporary kitchen.

2. Briefly discuss the use of fruit in the contemporary kitchen.

CHAPTER 9

DAIRY AND EGG PURCHASING AND IDENTIFICATION

Chapter Overview

A concentrated source of many nutrients, dairy products and eggs hold a prominent place on menus, on their own and as key ingredients in many preparations. Béchamel sauce, for example, is based on milk, and cream, crème fraîche, sour cream, and yogurt are used to finish sauces, to prepare salad dressings, and in many baked goods. Cheeses may be served as is, perhaps as a separate course with fruit, or as part of another dish. Fondue, raclette, and Welsh rarebit are classic dishes from around the world that feature cheese. And eggs appear not just on their own, in breakfast dishes to dessert soufflés, but in numerous sauces, especially emulsified ones such as hollandaise and mayonnaise.

Chapter Objectives

After reading and studying this chapter, you will be able to

➤ list the general guidelines for purchasing and storing dairy and eggs

➤ explain what is meant by pasteurization and homogenization of liquid dairy

➤ identify and classify dairy products according to the butterfat (or milkfat) content

➤ identify a variety of fermented and cultured milk products

➤ identify a variety of cheeses and group them according to milk type, texture, age, or ripening process

➤ identify the parts of an egg and list several uses and functions for whole eggs, egg yolks, and egg whites

➤ name the grades, sizes, and forms for eggs

Study Outline

Purchasing and Storage

Key Terms and Concepts

contamination	freshness	shelf life
dairy products	holding temperatures	wholesomeness
eggs	perishable	
flavor transfer	rotating stock	

Dairy Products

Key Terms and Concepts

age/aging
bacterial strain
blue cheese
blue-veined cheese
buffalo's milk
butter
butterfat
buttermilk
centrifuge
cheese
cheese foods
churned butter
condensed milk
cow's milk
cream
crème fraîche
cultured milk products
curdled milk
curds
dairy products
date stamp
dried powdered buttermilk
dry milk powder
evaporated milk
farmhouse-style cheeses
fat-free
fat-soluble vitamins
fermented milk products

fortification
fresh cheese
frozen dairy foods
frozen tofu
frozen yogurt
goat's milk
grating cheese
half-and-half
hard cheese
heavy cream
homogenization
ice cream
ice milk
light cream
"living" cheeses
low-fat milk
maturity
milk
milk products
milkfat
natural cheeses
nonfat milk
pasteurization
pasteurized cheeses
percentage of fat/milkfat
premium ice cream
processed cheeses
rennet

rind-ripened cheese
ripening
salted butter
semi-soft cheese
sheep's milk
sherbet
skim milk
soft cheese
sorbet
sour cream
sour milk
stabilization
stabilizers
starter
state and local government
    standards
sweet butter
sweet cream
tartaric acid
ultrapasteurization
unsalted butter
wax rind
whey
whipping cream
whole milk
yogurt

Cheese

Fresh cheese
Soft or rind-ripened cheese

Semisoft cheese
Hard cheese

Grating cheese
Blue-veined cheese

Eggs

Key Terms and Concepts

albumen
bulk eggs
chalazae
contamination
dried, powdered eggs
egg
egg substitutes
egg white
egg yolk
emulsifier
extra large eggs

fluid eggs
foam
food-borne illness
frozen eggs
grades
jumbo eggs
large eggs
lecithin
medium eggs
pasteurized egg
pee wee eggs

protein
raw eggs
safe handling
safe temperatures
salmonella enteritidis
  bacteria
shell egg
small eggs
U.S. Department of
  Agriculture (USDA)

- All eggs in the shell should be free from cracks, leaking, and obvious holes.
- Raw egg yolks are a potentially hazardous food due to the possible presence of *Salmonella enteritidis* bacteria. Salmonella bacteria are killed when the eggs are held at a temperature of at least 140°F (60°C) for a minimum of 3 1/2 minutes. The bacteria is also killed instantly at 160°F (71°C). Fried eggs or poached eggs with runny yolks should be prepared only at customer request.
- All foods containing eggs must be kept at safe temperatures throughout handling, cooking, and storage.

Egg Structure and Uses
Grading, Sizes, and Forms

Chapter 9 Exercises

True/False

Indicate whether each of the following statements is True (T) or False (F)

_____ 1. When fully ripe, a soft cheese should be nearly runny, with a full flavor.

_____ 2. Condensed milk is evaporated milk that has been sweetened.

_____ 3. Frozen yogurt and frozen tofu often contain stabilizers, a high percentage of fat, and a high sugar content.

_____ 4. The color of butter depends on the breed of the cow and the time of year.

_____ 5. Because of the risk of food-borne illness due to salmonella bacteria, fried or poached eggs with runny yolks should never be served to a customer.

_____ 6. Most low fat and skim milks are fortified to extend their shelf life.

_____ 7. Fresh cheeses and soft cheeses share similar characteristics and are generally used for the same purposes.

_____ 8. American cheese is a sliced processed cheese, such as Cheddar.

_____ 9. Some milks and creams are stabilized to make them more digestible for those persons who may be lactose intolerant.

_____ 10. Pasteurized eggs are used in preparations where the traditional recipe calls for raw eggs to prevent infection by the salmonella enteritidis bacteria.

Multiple Choice

1. Controlled fermentation is achieved by
   a. heating milk to a high temperature to kill bacteria and other organisms.
   b. forcing milk through a mesh to break up fat globules that are then dispersed evenly throughout the milk.
   c. adding vitamins and/or minerals, especially those that might have been removed.
   d. adding a bacterial strain to the milk product.

2. Pasteurization is the process of
   a. heating milk to a high temperature to kill bacteria and other organisms.
   b. forcing milk through a mesh to break up fat globules that are then dispersed evenly throughout the milk.
   c. adding vitamins and/or minerals, especially those that might have been removed.
   d. adding a bacterial strain to the milk product.

3. Fortification is the process of
   a. heating milk to a high temperature to kill bacteria and other organisms.
   b. forcing milk through a mesh to break up fat globules that are then dispersed evenly throughout the milk.
   c. adding vitamins and/or minerals, especially those that might have been removed.
   d. adding a bacterial strain to the milk product.

4. Homogenization is the process of
   a. heating milk to a high temperature to kill bacteria and other organisms.
   b. forcing milk through a mesh to break up fat globules that are then dispersed evenly throughout the milk.
   c. adding vitamins and/or minerals, especially those that might have been removed.
   d. adding a bacterial strain to the milk product.

5. In order to meet government standards, the percentage of milkfat in vanilla ice cream must be at least
   a. 2 percent.

b. 8 percent.
c. 10 percent.
d. 12 percent.

Fill in the Blank

1. In addition to adding flavor, the main reason salt is added to butter is to _____.

2. Yogurt is a cultured _____product. Sour cream is cultured _____
   ____. Crème fraîche is cultured _____.

3. Yogurt, sour cream, and buttermilk are all produced by inoculating milk or cream with
   _____which causes fermentation to begin. These products are said to
   be _____.

4. Natural cheeses are considered "living". The cheese keeps growing, developing, and aging to
   maturity or _____. When it spoils, it is said to be _____.

5. The blue veining in blue cheese is the result of _____.

Matching

_____ 1. whey
_____ 2. pasteurize
_____ 3. buttermilk
_____ 4. albumen
_____ 5. tartaric acid
_____ 6. homogenize

a. protein in egg white
b. to disperse fat globules evenly throughout milk
c. starter for cheese which causes milk to form curds
d. to heat milk to kill bacteria
e. fluid remaining when butter is churned
f. liquid remaining when milk forms curds during cheese production

Written/Short Answer

1. How should fresh milk and dairy products be stored?

_____

_____

_____

_____

2. How should eggs be stored?

_____

_____

_____

_____

3. Why is there such concern about eggs? What are some basic rules for safe handling of eggs and foods containing eggs?

_____

_____

_____

_____

4. What is the process of pasteurization and what is its purpose?

_____

_____

_____

_____

5. What types of ice cream and frozen dairy products are available and what are the government standards for these products?

_____

_____

_____

_____

6. What kinds of butter are available and what are the government standards?

_____

_____

_____

_____

7. How are fermented and cultured milk products produced?

_____

_____

_____

_____

Essay

1. What are some uses of eggs in culinary preparations?

2. What are the varieties of cheeses, the characteristics of each, and some possible uses for each?

CHAPTER **10**

DRY GOODS IDENTIFICATION

Chapter Overview

A broad spectrum of dry goods forms part of any food service operation's basic needs. Whole grains, meals, and flours; dried legumes; dried pasta and noodles; nuts and seeds; sugars, syrups, and other sweeteners; oils and shortenings; vinegars and condiments; coffee, tea, and other beverages; dry goods for baking; dried herbs and spices; and cooking wines, liqueurs, and cordials must be chosen, purchased, and stored with the same degree of care as fresh meats or produce.

Dry goods such as these are occasionally referred to as nonperishable goods. However, these ingredients, like perishable goods, lose quality over time. Keeping an adequate par stock on hand is essential to a smooth running operation, but having too much ties up unnecessary space and money. Rotating dry goods and observing a rule of "first in, first out" is just as important for dry goods as for more perishable foods.

Chapter Objectives

After reading and studying this chapter, you will be able to

➤ name the purchasing and storage guidelines for a number of dry goods and nonperishable items

➤ define dry goods

➤ explain and use the FIFO (first in, first out) system

➤ identify a variety of grains, meals and flours, dried legumes, and pastas

➤ select and use a variety of oils and shortenings for cooking, baking, and as an ingredient in sauces

➤ select and store a variety of vinegars and condiments

➤ identify, store, and handle a variety of nuts and seeds, dried fruits and vegetables

➤ identify, store, and handle various forms and varieties of salt and pepper

➤ select, identify, and properly store sugars, syrups, and other sweeteners, chocolate, extracts, and leaveners

➤ use appropriate guidelines to select, use, prepare, and store coffee, tea, and other beverages; wines, cordials, and liqueurs; and prepared, canned, and frozen foods

Study Outline

Purchasing and Storage

Key Terms and Concepts

dry goods
first in, first out (FIFO)

nonperishable goods
par stock

rotating stock

Grains, Meals, and Flours

Key Terms and Concepts

all-purpose flour
Arborio rice
barley
barley flour
barley meal
basmati rice
bran
bread flour
brown rice
buckwheat
bulgur wheat
cake flour
carnaroli rice
converted rice
corn
cornmeal
cornstarch
couscous
cracked grains
cracked wheat
cream of rice
farina

flour
fruit and seed of cereal
grasses
germ
glutinous rice
graham flour
grains
grinding
grits
hard wheat
hominy
hull
hulled/unhulled
Italian rice
kernels
masa
masa harina
milled/unmilled
millet
oat bran
oatmeal
oats

pastry flour
pearl barley
Piedmontese rice
polished/unpolished
pot barley
rice
rice flour
rye
Scotch barley
self-rising flour
semolina
soft wheat
sorghum
stone-ground grains
wheat
wheat berries
wheat flour
white rice
whole grains
whole wheat
whole wheat flour
wild rice

Wheat
Whole
Cracked
Bulgur

Semolina
Couscous
Farina

Bran
Germ

Wheat Flour
Whole or graham
All-purpose
Self-rising

Bread
Cake

Pastry

Rice

Brown	Basmati	Glutinous
White	Italian	Rice flour
Converted	Wild	

Corn

Hominy	Meal	Masa harina
Grits	Masa	Cornstarch

Barley

Pot or Scotch	Pearl
Barley meal	Barley flour

Oats

Oats	Oatmeal	Oat bran

Others

Buckwheat	Rye
Millet	Sorghum

Dried Legumes

Key Terms and Concepts

beans	fresh	pods
dried beans	legumes	seeds

Key Terms from Bean Chart

beans	flageolet	soybeans
adzuki beans	kidney beans	bean paste, soy
black beans	lentils	bean paste, hot
turtle beans	lima beans	bean paste, sweet/red
black-eyed peas	mung beans	miso
cannelini	navy beans	tofu (soybean curd)
chick-peas	pigeon peas	peas, fresh
fava beans	pinto beans	peas, dried
broad beans	soissons	

Dried Pasta and Noodles

Key Terms and Concepts

wheat flour	dried pasta
durum semolina	dried noodles

Key Terms from Pasta and Noodles Chart

(Italian/English)
acini di pepe/peppercorns
anelli/rings
arrowroot vermicelli
bucatini
cannelloni/large pipes
capellini/hair
cavatelli
cellophane noodles
conchiglie/shells
couscous
ditali/thimbles
egg flakes
egg noodles

elbow macaroni
farfalle/butterflies
fedelini
fettuccine
fiochetti/bowties
fusilli/twists
lasagne
linguine
mafalda
manicotti/small muffs
mostaccioli/small mustaches
orecchiette/ears
orzo/barley
pappardelle

pastina/tiny pasta
penne/quills or pens
rice noodles
rigatoni
rotelle/wheels
rotini/cartwheels
soba (Japanese)
somen (Japanese)
spaghetti/little strings
tagliatelle
tubetti/tubes
udon (Japanese)
vermicelli
ziti/bridegrooms

Oils and Shortening

Key Terms and Concepts

almond oil
baking fat
blended oils
blended shortening
butter-flavored oils
butter-flavored shortening
canola oil
clarified
coconut oil
cold pressed
cold-pressed olive oil
cooking oils
corn oil
cottonseed oil
dark sesame oil

extra-virgin olive oil
filtered
frying fats
grapeseed oil
hazelnut oil
hydrogenated/hydrogenation
lard
light sesame oil
nut oil
oil
oil sprays
olive oil
olive-pomace oil
peanut oil
rapeseed oil

refined oil
safflower oil
salad oil
sesame oil
shortening
smoking point
soybean oil
sunflower oil
thermally refined olive oil
vegetable oil
vegetable shortening
virgin olive oil
walnut oil

Nuts and Seeds

Key Terms and Concepts

blanched
celery seed
chopped
fennel seed
fruits of trees
in the shell

nut butters
nuts
paste
pumpkin seed
rancid
roasted

seeds
shelled
sliced
slivered
spices
sunflower seed

Key Terms from Nuts and Seeds Chart

almond
Brazil
cashew
chestnut
coconut
hazelnut

macadamia
peanut
pecan
pine nut
pistachio
poppy seeds

pumpkin seeds
sesame seeds
sunflower seeds
walnut

Dried Herbs and Spices

Key Terms and Concepts

chemically dried vegetables
dried fruit
dried herbs

ground spices
low-moisture fruits and
   vegetables

spice blends
vacuum-dried vegetables
whole spices

Salt and Pepper

Key Terms and Concepts

bay salt
black peppercorns
canning salt
cayenne
chile flakes
cracked pepper
crushed pepper
curing salt
Diamond Crystal kosher salt
green peppercorns
ground pepper

Hungarian paprika
iodized salt
kosher salt
light salt
mignonette
paprika
pickling salt
pink peppercorns
popcorn salt
red pepper flakes
rock salt

salt curing
salt substitutes
sea salt
shot pepper
superfine grain
Szechwan peppercorns
table salt
Telicherry peppercorn
white peppercorns
whole peppercorns

Sugars, Syrups, and Other Sweeteners

Key Terms and Concepts

10x
bar sugar
blackstrap molasses
brown sugar
confectioners'
corn syrup
creamed honey
cube sugar
Demerara
flavored syrups

honey
honeycomb
liquefied sugar
maple syrup
molasses
muscovado
preserving sugar
refined sugar
sugars
sulfured/unsulfured molasses

syrups
table sugar
treacle
turbinado
white, coarse
white, granulated
white, lump
white, superfine

Sugars

Brown	Turbinado	White, superfine
Muscovado	White, coarse	Confectioners'
Demerara	White, granulated	White, lump

Syrups

Corn	Treacle	Molasses
Maple	Flavored	Honey

Chocolate

Key Terms and Concepts

bloom	cocoa beans	white chocolate
chocolate	cocoa butter	
chocolate liquor	cocoa powder	

Key Terms from Chocolate Chart

Chocolate liquor	Chocolate, unsweetened	Chocolate, coating
Cocoa butter	(bitter/baking)	(couverture)
Cocoa	Chocolate, bittersweet	Confectionery coating
Cocoa, Dutch-process	Chocolate, semisweet	Chocolate, white
Cocoa, breakfast	Chocolate, sweet	Chocolate syrup
Cocoa, low-fat	Chocolate, milk	Chocolate sauce
Cocoa, instant		Carob

Chocolate and Related Products

Miscellaneous Dry Goods

Key Terms and Concepts

arrowroot	cornstarch	jams
baking powder	decaffeinated coffee	leaveners
baking soda	emulsion	liqueur
black tea	espresso	mustard
canned juice	extracts	olives
canned products	fermentation	pickles
cappuccino	FIFO rule	relish
chemical leaveners	file gumbo powder	sodium bicarbonate
coffee	fortified wines	tea
coffee beans	frozen goods	thickeners
condiments	frozen juice	vacuum-packed coffee
convenience foods	gelatin	vinegars
cordial	herbal tea	wine

Thickeners
Arrowroot   File Gumbo Powder
Cornstarch   Gelatin

Coffee, tea, and other beverages
Wines, cordials, and liqueurs
Prepared, canned, and frozen foods

Chapter 10 Exercises

True/False

Indicate whether each of the following statements is True (T) or False (F)

_____ 1.   Pink peppercorns are not true peppercorns; they are berries from a type of rose plant.

_____ 2.   Sea and bay salts from different areas of the world taste different and generally have more complex flavors than kosher salt.

_____ 3.   Canning and pickling salts have a grayish tint from the usually harmless impurities they contain. Those that are safe for consumption are marked as edible.

_____ 4.   Fortified wines are more delicate than table wines and must be stored in the refrigerator.

_____ 5.   Stone grinding of grains may be preferred because the grinding is done at a lower temperature than other methods and so the grains retain more of their nutritional value.

_____ 6.   As legumes age, they take a shorter amount of time to cook.

_____ 7.   Curing salts are a blend of 94 percent sodium nitrite and 6 percent salt.

_____ 8.   Good-quality dried pastas from wheat flour are customarily made from durum semolina.

_____ 9.   Somen and udon noodles are wheat flour noodles used in Japanese cooking.

_____ 10.   Extra-virgin olive oil and virgin olive oil must be produced without the use of heat.

Multiple Choice

1. Bulgur is a type of
   a. corn.
   b. rice.
   c. wheat.
   d. barley.

2. Basmati is a type of
   a. buckwheat.
   b. rice.
   c. wheat.
   d. barley.

3. Kasha is a type of
   a. corn.
   b. wheat.
   c. buckwheat.
   d. barley.

4. Of the following rices, which provides the most nutritional value?
   a. Brown.
   b. White.
   c. Converted.
   d. Arborio.

5. Couscous is made from
   a. wheat flour.
   b. rice flour.
   c. mung bean starch.
   d. semolina.

Fill in the Blank

1. Baking fats or shortenings are usually _____ to enable absorption of more sugar in baked goods.

2. Olive oils that are produced without the use of heat, are said to be _____.

3. The light, aromatic yellow oil that is a by-product of wine making is _____.

4. The coarse salt that has a gray tint and is used to hand-crank ice cream or as a bed for shellfish is called _____.

5. Superfine white sugar is also known as _____. 10X sugar is another name for _____.

Matching
_____ 1. pink peppercorn
_____ 2. treacle
_____ 3. Szechwan peppercorn
_____ 4. legume
_____ 5. peanut
_____ 6. farfalle

a. dried bean
b. root from a leguminous plant
c. by-product of sugar making
d. pasta made from wheat flour
e. berry from the baies rose plant
f. berry from the prickly ash tree

Written/Short Answer
1. What is a par stock?

_____

_____

_____

_____

2. Generally, how should dry goods be stored?

_____

_____

_____

_____

3. How do you determine which oil or fat to use for which purpose?

_____

_____

_____

_____

4. What is the smoking point and why is it important to know the smoking point?

_____

_____

_____

_____

5. How should nuts and seeds be stored?

_____

_____

_____

_____

6. How should dried herbs and spices be purchased and stored?

_____

_____

_____

_____

7. How should chocolate and chocolate products be stored?

_____

_____

_____

_____

Essay

1. Discuss the use of grains in the kitchen and the various forms of whole and milled grains.

2. Discuss the use of prepared, canned and frozen foods in the professional kitchen.

CHAPTER **11**

MISE EN PLACE FOR STOCKS, SAUCES, AND SOUPS

Chapter Overview

Throughout your culinary career, you may use different types of aromatics and flavorings and thickeners. As part of your everyday preparation (mise en place), you will be called upon to prepare bouquet garni, sachet d'épices, mirepoix, clarified butter, roux, pure starch slurries, and liaisons. Having a full and well-prepared mise en place on hand before preparing stocks, sauces or soup will help you to be faster and more efficient in your work. These basic components must be prepared with the same care as the dishes in which you will use them.

Chapter Objectives

After reading and studying this chapter, you will be able to

➤ Define and use bouquet garni and sachet d'épices, listing common ingredients for each and standard cooking times for flavor extraction.

➤ Prepare mirepoix and be able to describe common ingredients and their handling and name several mirepoix variations. Cook mirepoix by either sweating or browning to affect flavors and colors in finished dishes.

➤ Explain the uses for roux and name the basic colors of roux; express the basic ratio for roux as a weight; combine roux and a liquid properly.

➤ Prepare clarified butter and describe its appropriate or common uses.

➤ Identify a variety of pure starches and their characteristics, use them to prepare a slurry, and substitute starches of different thickening powers in recipes using a standard formula.

➤ Name the ingredients in a liaison, describe the effect of a liaison on a dish. Hold dishes finished with a liaison properly for safety and quality.

Study Outline

Key concepts and terms

mise en place	pinçage	ghee
aromatic	white mirepoix	pure starch slurry
bouquet garni	matignon	liaison
sachet d'épices	batutto	coagulate
mirepoix	soffrito	tempering
sweat	roux	
caramelize	clarified butter	

Bouquet Garni and Sachet d'épices

Function of these aromatics

Ingredients for bouquet, illustrations of preparation, page 235

Ingredients for sachet

How and when to add to a dish

Mirepoix, pages 236-237

Function of roux

Amount of roux to flavor 1 gall. liquid

Ingredient preparation for mirepoix

- ➤ trimming, etc.
- ➤ cut to size
- ➤ sweating for white stocks, sauces, soups
- ➤ cook to brown for brown stocks, sauces, soups
- ➤ tomato paste or puree in mirepoix
- ➤ pinçage, illustration page 237

Mirepoix variations, page 237

- ➤ white mirepoix
- ➤ Cajun trinity
- ➤ matignon (edible mirepoix)
- ➤ Batutto

Roux, pages 238-239

Ingredients for roux

Preparing roux (stovetop or oven), illustrations page 239

Colors of roux

Combining roux with liquid

- ➤ add cool roux to hot liquid
- ➤ add cool liquid to hot roux
- ➤ avoid temperature extremes

Clarified Butter, page 240

Purpose of clarifying butter

Uses for clarified butter

Method for preparing, illustration page 240

Ghee defined

Pure starch slurries, page 241

Types of starches used

➢ arrowroot

➢ cornstarch

➢ tapioca

➢ potato starch

➢ rice flour

Blending starch with liquid to make slurry

To substitute a pure starch for roux, use the following formula, page 241

Liaison

Purpose of liaison

Ingredients for liaison
Blending and tempering liaison, illustration page 242
Holding dishes finished with liaison

Chapter 11 Exercises

Matching

_____ 1. Liaison

_____ 2. Matignon

_____ 3. Roux

_____ 4. Mirepoix

_____ 5. Slurry

_____ 6. Bouquet garni

_____ 7. Sachet d'épices

_____ 8. Clarified butter

_____ 9. Tempering

_____ 10. Arrowroot

_____ 11. Mise en place

a. An edible mirepoix intended to be served as part of a finished dish.

b. A starch dissolved in a cold liquid.

c. A mixture of both egg yolks and cream, used to both thicken and enrich sauces and soups.

d. A combination of rough, chopped aromatic vegetables, used to flavor stocks, soups, braises, and stews.

e. A combination of herbs and vegetables, tied in a bundle, used to flavor savory preparations.

f. Cooked fat and flour; often prepared in advance in large quantities.

g. A "bag of spices" that is removed and discarded after enough flavor has been given.

h. Butter heated so that the milk solids and water separate from the butterfat.

i. Combining a ingredients in such a way that temperature extremes are avoided.

k. All ingredients, preparations, and equipment necessary for a dish

Multiple Choice

1. A mixture of egg yolks and cream used to thicken a sauce is called a(n)
    a. béchamel.
    b. liaison.
    c. tournant.
    d. egg wash.

2. Adding a portion of a hot liquid to a liaison to keep it from "scrambling" is called
    a. rendering.
    b. tempering.
    c. clarifying.
    d. dissolving.
    e. blanching.

3. What is the difference between a matignon and a mirepoix?
    a. Mirepoix is rough cut, whereas matignon is uniformly cut.
    b. Mirepoix is strained from a preparation and a matignon is left in to be eaten as part of the dish.
    c. Matignon contains bacon or ham, whereas mirepoix is meatless.
    d. The vegetables in a matignon are peeled, but in a mirepoix they may be unpeeled.
    e. All of the above.

4. A bouquet garni is used to prepare
    a. roasts.
    b. spice blends.
    c. flavored oils and vinegars.
    d. stocks, soups, sauces, stews, and braised foods.

5. Mirepoix is added to stocks, soups, and sauces as they simmer to enhance
    a. aroma and flavor.
    b. color.
    c. texture.
    d. nutrients.

True/False

_____ 1. A liaison is a modified starch dissolved in a cold liquid.

_____ 2. The ratio of roux to liquid for a medium consistency sauce is 12-16 ounces per gallon

_____ 3. Mirepoix is an essential ingredient in all soups.

_____ 4. When tempering a liaison it is okay to add the egg yolks directly into the hot liquid.

_____ 5. Clarified butter is butter in which the milk solids have separated from the butterfat.

Fill in the blank

1. When combining roux with a liquid, be sure that their individual temperatures are
   _____.

2. Clarified butter can be heated to a higher temperature than whole butter without burning or breaking down because the _____, which scorch easily, have been removed.

3. A liaison is prepared from 3 parts _____ and 1 part _____.

4. Mirepoix can be prepared by either _____ or _____.

5. Cooking tomato paste or puree to develop a good flavor is known as _____.

Written/Short Answer

1. Define the following:
   a. Aromatic

   _____

   _____

   b. Mirepoix

   _____

   _____

   c. Sachet d'épices

   _____

   _____

   d. Tempering

   _____

   _____

2. Discuss the use of clarified butter as a cooking medium versus melted butter or various oils.

   _____

   _____

3. How is roux combined with a simmering liquid?

_____

_____

_____

4. What is the best sequence for adding the ingredients in a mirepoix to the pan when cooking the mirepoix in fat?

_____

_____

_____

5. Recipes and cookbooks may refer to something as an aromatic. Define aromatic as it relates to cooking and briefly explain when an ingredient is considered an aromatic, rather than a main flavoring ingredient?

_____

_____

_____

_____

_____

_____

6. There are many shortcuts used by experienced chefs. Describe how you might organize the work involved in preparing the items included in this chapter and what short cuts you might try and why.

_____

_____

_____

_____

_____

_____

CHAPTER 12

Chapter Overview

Stocks are among the most basic preparations found in any professional kitchen. In fact, they are referred to in French as fonds de cuisine, or the foundations of cooking. Stocks are made by gently simmering meaty bones, trim, and/or vegetables in a liquid to extract their flavor, aroma, color, body, and nutritive value and then used to prepare sauces, soups, stews, and braises and as a cooking medium for vegetables and grains.

Chapter Objectives

After reading and studying this chapter, you will be able to

➢ describe the characteristics and quality indicators for brown stock, white stock, fumets, essences, and court bouillon

➢ select and prepare the ingredients and equipment necessary to produce stocks

➢ name the correct method for producing various stocks

➢ prepare, hold, and reheat stocks for the best flavor, body, color

➢ follow safe food handling practices for stocks

➢ define various stocks and related preparations, including remouillage, nage, and glace

➢ explain how to test and evaluate commercially prepared bases

Study Outline

Key Concepts and Terms

white stock	nage	glace
brown stock	sweating	commercially prepared base
fumet	smothering	conditioning a pan
essence	browning	cooling stock safely
court bouillon	remouillage	

Select and Prepare the Ingredients and Equipment, page 245

Meat and Fish Bones

➢ Any wholesome trim from fabrication, if available, to further bolster flavor.

➢ Cut bones into 3-inch lengths for quicker and more thorough extraction of flavor, gelatin, and nutritive value.

➢ If bones are purchased frozen, thaw them before using to make stock.

➢ Rinse well.

➢ All bones, fresh or frozen, before putting them into the stockpot, to remove blood and other impurities that can compromise the quality of the stock.

➢ For brown stocks, prepare the bones and trim by roasting them first; for more information, see page 252.

➢ For fish stocks, use only bones from lean flatfish like sole and turbot. Bones from oily fish like salmon and tuna are too strongly flavored and have too high a fat content. The entire fish carcass, including the head if it is very fresh, can be used. If including the head, cut away the gills first. They will discolor the stock and give it an off taste. Ice fish bones overnight to extract blood, which can cloud the stock.

➢ Trim and cut mirepoix to a size that will allow for good flavor extraction. A ½-inch slice or dice is good for simmering time of 1 hour. Cut vegetables larger or smaller for longer or shorter simmering times. The mirepoix and tomato paste called for in brown stocks are usually roasted or sautéed until browned before being added to the stock.

Sachet d' épices or Bouquet Garni (pages 234–235) *Containing Aromatics Suited to the Type of Stock Being Made.*

Pots used for stocks are usually taller than they are wide

➢ Creates a smaller surface area so the evaporation rate is minimized during simmering.

➢ Some stockpots have spigots at the bottom that can be used to remove the finished stock without disturbing the bones. Steam-jacketed kettles are often used to produce large quantities of stock.

Court bouillons, fumets, and essences that do not have long simmering times can be prepared in rondeaus or other wide shallow pots. Tilting kettles are used when available for large-scale production.

Ladles or skimmers

Cheesecloth, sieves, and colanders are used to separate the bones and vegetables from the stock.

Thermometer

Containers for cooling as well as storing

Chicken Stock, illustrated on pages 246-249

General Guidelines for Working with Stocks

Storing Stock

➢ Cool and store them the right way (see page 64–65).

➢ To check a stock before using it, reboil a small amount and taste it. The aroma should be appealing but not overly pungent or sour.

Remouillage

Some chefs like to reserve the simmered bones and mirepoix to prepare a remouillage by simmering them a second time. This secondary stock can be used as the liquid for stocks, broths, as a cooking medium, or reduced to a glace.

Glace

Glace is a highly reduced stock or remouillage. As a result of continued reduction, the stock acquires a jellylike or syrupy consistency and its flavor becomes highly concentrated. Glaces are used to bolster the flavor of other foods, particularly sauces. When they are reconstituted with water, they may also serve as a sauce base in much the same way as a commercially prepared base.

Commercial Bases

Bases are available in

➢ highly reduced forms, similar to the classic glace de viande, or

➢ dehydrated (powdered or cubed).

Having decided that a base meets your standards for quality and cost, learn how to make any adjustments you find necessary. For example, you might sweat or roast more vegetables and simmer them in a diluted base, perhaps along with browned trim, to make a rich brown sauce.

Chapter 12 Exercises

Matching

1. Dressing
2. Mie de pain
3. Eggwash

4. Carryover cooking
5. Standard breading procedure
6. Aromatics

_____ a. Herbs, spices, and vegetables used to enhance the flavor and fragrance of food

_____ b. Stuffing that is baked separately, outside of the meat, poultry, or fish

_____ c.   Fresh bread crumbs

_____ d.   The process of dusting food items in flour, dipping in eggwash, and then coating with breading

_____ e.   A mixture of beaten eggs, egg whites or yolks, and liquid used as a coating

_____ f.   The phenomenon which causes food to continue cooking even after it is removed from the heat source

Multiple Choice

1. Chapelure is the French term for
   a. standard breading procedure.
   b. dry bread crumbs.
   c. carry over cooking.
   d. stuffing prepared with forcemeat.

2. Which items are generally associated with marinades?
   a. Eggwash, flour, bread crumbs
   b. Mie de pain, acid, aromatics
   c. Oils, chapelure, aromatics
   d. Acids, oils, aromatics

3. The proper sequence for standard breading procedure is
   a. bread crumbs, eggwash, flour.
   b. flour, eggwash, bread crumbs.
   c. eggwash, flour and bread crumbs combined.
   d. flour and bread crumbs combined, eggwash.

4. Stuffing which is baked separately from the main item rather than stuffed inside is known as
   a. forcemeat stuffing.
   b. chapelure.
   c. binding.
   d. dressing.

5. The purpose of the standard breading procedure is
   a. to create a crisp crust on fried food.
   b. to prevent cross-contamination of food items.
   c. to increase the size and bulk of the food.
   d. to add protein.

True/False

Indicate whether the each of the following statements is true (T) or False (F)

_____ 1.   Leftover flour, eggwash, and bread crumbs from standard breading should be refrigerated if they are to be used again.

_____ 2.   Tender or delicate foods should not be marinated.

_____ 3. Grains should always be cooked and cooled before being added to stuffings.

_____ 4. Stuffing prepared for roasted birds and baked separately is called dressing.

_____ 5. Seeds and spices should not be toasted on the stovetop, as they tend to burn easily.

_____ 6. Only the yolks of eggs should be used to prepare eggwash.

_____ 7. Grain stuffings can be seasoned, moistened, and bound in a manner similar to bread crumb stuffings.

_____ 8. The purpose of standard breading is to create a crisp crust on fried food.

_____ 9. Items such as cornflakes and coconut may be used in addition to or in place of bread crumbs in the standard breading procedure.

_____ 10. A chef should not rely on touch as a gauge for measuring doneness of meat.

Fill in the Blank

1. _____, including wine and vinegar, are used in marinades to change the texture and flavor of foods.

2. _____ refers to the temperature an item reaches which combines cooking temperature with carryover cooking.

3. Seeds and spices are often _____ to enhance their flavor.

4. Herbs, spices, and vegetables used to enhance the flavor and fragrance of food are known as _____.

5. _____ is the French term for fresh bread crumbs. Dry bread crumbs are called _____.

Written/Short Answer

1. Explain the various ingredients for the standard breading procedure and their proper application.

_____

_____

_____

_____

2. What is carryover cooking and what factors might affect it?

_____

_____

_____

_____

_____

3. Why are seeds and spices toasted, and how is it done?

_____

_____

_____

_____

_____

4. What are the ingredients in a simple stuffing? In a more complex stuffing?

_____

_____

_____

_____

_____

5. How is marinating time determined?

_____

_____

_____

_____

6. Appropriate aromatics and their preparation methods include

_____

_____

_____

7. How is glaçe de viande prepared? What are some uses for glaçe?

_____

_____

_____

_____

8. The most important steps for producing a good stock are:

_____

_____

_____

_____

CHAPTER **13**

Chapter Overview

Sauces are often considered one of the greatest tests of a chef's skill. The successful pairing of a sauce with a food demonstrates technical expertise, an understanding of the food, and the ability to judge and evaluate a dish's flavors, textures, and colors.

Chapter Objectives

After reading and studying this chapter, you will be able to

➢ Describe the characteristics and quality indicators for brown sauce, white sauce, tomato sauce, hollandaise, and beurre blanc

➢ Select and prepare the ingredients and equipment necessary to produce sauces

➢ Name the correct method for producing various sauces

➢ Prepare, hold, and reheat sauces for the best flavor, texture, color

➢ Follow safe food handling practices for sauces

➢ Explain how and why sauces are combined with other foods

➢ Select sauces that are appropriate for specific foods, cooking techniques, or serving situations

Study Outline

Brown Sauce

Key Terms and Concepts

brown sauce	pincé	fortified wine
Espagnole sauce	deglaze	garnish
Demi-glace	finishing with butter (monter	
jus de veau lié	au beurre)	
reduction-style sauces	reduction	

Select and Prepare the Ingredients and Equipment

Base stock, usually Brown Veal Stock, page 252

Bones and trim, cut them into small pieces for better and faster flavor development
➤ Note: If the stock is extremely flavorful, additional bones and trim may not be necessary.

Mirepoix, mushroom trimmings, herbs, garlic, or shallots.
Thickener, if necessary:
➤ roux (see page 238–239) or

➤ pure starch slurry (see page 241).

Pot that is wider than it is tall.

White Sauce

Key Terms and Concepts

white sauce	bechamel	scorching
velouté	combining roux and liquid	non-reactive pans

Select and Prepare the Ingredients and Equipment

Chicken Velouté, illustrated pages 263-265

Tomato Sauce

Key Terms and Concepts

plum tomatoes	correcting harsh or bitter
fresh and canned tomatoes	flavors
puréeing	weeping

Select and Prepare the Ingredients and Equipment

Fresh or canned tomatoes
➤ When fresh tomatoes are at their peak, it may be a good idea to use them exclusively. At other times of the year, good-quality canned tomatoes are a better choice.

➤ Plum tomatoes, sometimes referred to as Romas, are generally preferred for tomato sauces because they have a high ratio of flesh to skin and seeds.

Tomato paste is sometimes added to the sauce as well.

Choices for additional flavoring ingredients

➤ mirepoix

➤ garlic and onions. Still others call for the inclusion of a

➤ ham bone or other smoked pork bones

➤ fresh and/or dried herbs

Heavy-gauge pot that is made of nonreactive materials such as stainless steel or anodized aluminum

If the sauce is to be pureéd

➤ food mill

➤ blender

➤ food processor

➤ immersion blender

Tomato Sauce, illustrated pages 270-271

Hollandaise Sauce

Key Terms and Concepts

emulsion sauce
reduction
pasteurized eggs

salmonella and safe handling
    of eggs
holding a warm sauce

Select and Prepare the Ingredients and Equipment

➤ melted whole butter or clarified butter(about 145°F/63 C)

➤ egg yolks, pasteurized if desired

➤ acidic ingredient, which can be either a vinegar reduction or lemon juice or, also provides the water necessary to form an emulsion

Hollandaise Sauce illustrated pages 276-278

Beurre Blanc

Key Terms and Concepts

beurre blanc
reduction

cuisson (from shallow-poaching)
reduced heavy cream

Select and Prepare the Ingredients and Equipment

➢ Unsalted butter (Check the butter carefully for a rich, sweet, creamy texture and aroma. Cube the butter and keep it cool or at room temperature.)

➢ Standard reduction for a beurre blanc made from dry white wine and shallots. (When prepared as part of a shallow-poached dish, the cooking liquid is cooked down to become the reduction, see pages 502-503.)

Other ingredients often used in the reduction include

➢ vinegar or citrus juice

➢ chopped herbs including tarragon, basil, chives, or chervil;

➢ cracked peppercorns

➢ garlic or ginger; lemongrass; saffron; and other flavoring ingredients.

Reduced heavy cream is occasionally added to stabilize the emulsion.

Pan is of a non-reactive metal wider than it is tall

If you choose to strain either the reduction or the finished sauce, you will need a sieve.

Beurre Blanc, illustrated pages 281-282

The Purpose of Sauces

Most sauces have more than one function in a dish. A sauce that adds a counterpoint flavor, for example, may also introduce textural and visual appeal. Sauces generally serve one or more of the following purposes:

➢ Introduce complementary or counterpoint flavors: Sauces that are classically paired with particular foods illustrate this function.

➢ Add moisture or succulence. A sauce can add moisture to naturally lean foods (e.g., poultry, fish), or when using cooking techniques that tend to have a drying effect, such as grilling or sautéing.

➢ Add visual interest: A sauce can enhance a dish's appearance by adding luster and sheen.

➢ Enhance flavors: A sauce that includes a flavor complementary to a food brings out the flavor of that food.

➢ Adjust texture: Many sauces include a garnish that adds texture to the finished dish.

Sauce Pairing

➢ Suitable for the style of service

➢ Matched to the main ingredient's cooking technique

➢ Appropriate for the flavor of the food with which it is paired:

Guidelines for Plating Sauces

➢ Maintain the temperature of the sauce: Check the temperature of the sauce, of the food being sauced, and of the plate. Be sure that hot sauces are extremely hot, warm emulsions sauces warm, and cold sauces cold.

➢ Consider the texture of the food being served.

➢ Avoid adding too much sauce to the plate: Spoon enough sauce on the plate for every bite of the sauced food but not so much that the dish looks swamped.

Chapter 13 Exercises

True/False

Indicate whether the each of the following statements is true (T) or False (F)

_____ 1.   Espagnole sauce is an essential ingredient in tomato sauce.

_____ 2.   The procedure for holding a beurre blanc sauce is the same as for bechamel sauce.

_____ 3.   A vin blanc sauce is a derivative of a Beurre Blanc Sauce.

_____ 4.   The purpose of a sauce is to complement, never contrast with, a particular food.

Multiple Choice

1.   Which of the following is true about sauces?
   a.   They add calories to a dish.
   b.   They detract from a dish's appearance.
   c.   They are made from butter and cream.
   d.   They should always be served extremely hot.
   e.   They add flavor and moisture to a dish.

2.   A demi-glace is made with what stock?
   a.   brown veal stock
   b.   milk
   c.   vegetable stock
   d.   any white stock
   e.   all of the above

3.   A demi-glace is made from

    c.   equal parts tomato sauce and Espagnole sauce reduced by half.

    b.   equal parts brown veal stock and velout reduced by half.

    a.   equal parts Espagnole sauce and white stock reduced by half.

    d.   any of the above.

    e.   none of the above.

4. A béchamel sauce is

    a.   cream with the addition of white roux.

    b.   the basis for all cream soups.

    c.   a derivative of velouté.

    d.   a grand sauce.

    e.   all of the above.

5. Sauce Espagnole is

    a.   the same as brown stock.

    b.   the same as demi-glace.

    c.   the same as brown sauce.

    d.   thickened by reduction.

    e.   the classical term for jus lié.

Fill in the Blank

1. _____ is a white sauce made by thickening white with a blond roux.

2. Hollandaise sauce should have a rich flavor of _____ and _____.

3. To prepare a _____, thicken drippings with cornstarch or arrowroot slurry.

4. Béchamel _____ is a white sauce made by thickening with.

Written/Short Answer

1. Name the characteristics of sauces.

_____

_____

_____

_____

CHAPTER **14**

Soups

Chapter Overview

Soup is a good vehicle for making use of wholesome trim from other kitchen operations. They can be hearty, as is the case with regional specialties: chowders, gumbos, thick vegetable or bean soups. They can also be smooth and suave: cream of mushroom, broccoli, or celery.

Chapter Objectives

After reading and studying this chapter, you will be able to

➢ Understand the basic ingredients and their functions in a soup.

➢ Understand how to properly cook, finish, garnish, reheat, adjust consistency, and degrease clear and thick soups.

➢ Prepare and evaluate the quality of clear soups, including consommés, broths, and clear vegetable soups.

➢ Prepare and evaluate the quality of thick soups, including purees, cream soups, and bisques.

➢ Serve hot and cold soups in the correct manner.

Study Outline

Key terms

bisque	broth	consommé julienne
clear vegetable soup	gazpacho	consommé printanier
consommé	chowder	consommé royal
puree	raft	
cream soup	consommé célèstine	

Chapter 14 Exercises

Matching

_____ 1. Bisque

_____ 2. Clear vegetable soup

_____ 3. Consommé

_____ 4. Puree

_____ 5. Cream soup

_____ 6. Broth

_____ 7. Gazpacho

_____ 8. Chowder

_____ 9. Raft

_____ 10. Consommé célèstine

_____ 11. Consommé julienne

a. A strong crystal clear broth or stock that has been clarified.

b. A somewhat thick and course soup based on dried peas, lentils, or beans or other starchy vegetables.

c. A chilled soup based on raw vegetables.

d. Based on a clear broth or stock with the vegetables cut into an appropriate and uniform size.

e. A rich, flavorful soup based on meats prepared with water or stock.

f. A thick soup invariably containing potatoes.

g. Béchamel- or velouté-based soup, finished with cream or a liaison.

h. Traditionally based on crustaceans and shares characteristics with both purees and cream soups.

i. Mass formed by clarification ingredients

j. Consommé lightly thickened with tapioca and garnishes with julienne of crêpes mixed with chopped truffles or herbs.

k. Consommé garnished with julienne of carrot, leek, turnip, celery, and cabbage, plus green peas, and chiffonade of sorrel and chervil.

Multiple Choice

1. The process of enriching a broth or stock and transforming it into a crystal-clear consommé is called
   a. degreasing.
   b. clarifying.
   c. spatzli.
   d. skimming.
   e. none of the above.

2. Which of the following soups are not considered clear soups?
   a. Broth
   b. Consommé
   c. Clear vegetable soup
   d. Bisque
   e. None of the above

3. A vegetable-based bisque is prepared in the same manner as a
   a. chowder.
   b. vichyssoise.
   c. consommé.
   d. cream soup.
   e. none of the above.

4. When is the best time to add cream to a cream soup?
   a. Immediately after it is pureed
   b. When the main flavoring components are added
   c. After it has come to a full boil
   d. Just before service
   e. Any of the above

5. Because a velvety-smooth texture is critical to all cream soups, what must be done?
   a. Use a consommé instead of a stock
   b. Use a veloute base as opposed to a bchamel
   c. Strain the soup
   d. Finish the cream soup with a liaison
   e. None of the above

True/False
Indicate whether the each of the following statements is true (T) or False (F)

_____ 1. Broths and clear vegetable soups characteristically have some droplets of fat on the surface.

_____ 2. Simmering a prepared consommé makes it easier to lift away the congealed fat surface.

_____ 3. A bisque that is properly made will have a slightly grainy texture.

Fill in the Blank
1. Clear vegetable soups should have a full flavor and be somewhat _____ than broths.
2. A cloudy consommé is most often the result of _____ the soup.
3. Cream soups should have the approximate body, consistency, and texture of

   _____.

4. The major distinction between broths and stocks is that broths are intended to be served

   _____.

5. _____ form the basis of most soups.

Written/Short Answer

1. Describe the procedure for finishing and garnishing soups.

   _____

   _____

   _____

2. Describe the procedure for reheating thick and clear soups.

   _____

   _____

   _____

3. What are the three basic types of soups? Give two examples of each.

_____

_____

_____

4. Briefly describe what garnishing can accomplish in soups.

_____

_____

_____

5. What qualities should a well-prepared broth have?

_____

_____

_____

6. Briefly describe how a consommé is clarified.

_____

_____

_____

7. What qualities should a well-prepared consommé have?

_____

_____

_____

8. What qualities should a well-prepared clear vegetable soup have?

_____

_____

_____

9. What qualities should a well-prepared cream soup have?

_____

_____

_____

10. What qualities should a well-prepared puree soup have?

_____

_____

_____

11. What qualities should a well-prepared bisque have?

_____

_____

_____

CHAPTER **15**

MISE EN PLACE FOR MEATS, POULTRY, AND FISH

Chapter Overview

Basic preparations and techniques used to prepare a variety of meats, poultry, and fish are fundamental to the development of a good flavor, color, and texture in any dish. The ability to select and prepare a variety of seasonings, stuffings, and coatings allows the chef to vary basic dishes to suit the season, a region, or ethnic cuisine. A chef who can determine the exact point when meats, poultry, or fish are properly cooked can greatly increase the quality of any dish.

Chapter Objectives

After reading and studying this chapter, you will be able to

➢   Select and prepare a variety of seasonings, including salt and pepper as well as spice and herb blends.

➢   Toast seeds and spices both on top of the stove and in the oven

➢   Name the various types of marinades and use them to achieve the desired effect.

➢   List the functions of a variety of stuffings.

➢   Prepare stuffings properly and combine them with foods safely.

➢   Select and prepare ingredients for standard breadings and name some of the variations on standard breading.

➢   Name the various tests for doneness when preparing meats, poultry, and fish.

➢   Explain carryover cooking and how it affects the doneness of meats, poultry, and fish dishes.

Study Outline

Seasonings, pages 346-47

Key concepts and terms

aromatics	toasting seeds and spices	acid
coatings	in the oven	aromatics (spice, herbs,
dry rub	on the stovetop	vegetables)
marinade	herb coatings	marinating times
spice and herb blends	dry rubs	liquid marinades
salt and pepper	marinades	
spice and herb blends	oil	

Stuffings, page 348

Key concepts and terms

dressing
forcemeat
proper handling for food safety

Stuffing
➤ simple stuffings

➤ complex stuffings

➤ bread stuffings

➤ grain-based stuffings

➤ forcemeat stuffings

Dressings
➤ Precooked ingredients must be cooled to 40°f/4°c before being combined with other ingredients

➤ Finished mixture should be chilled well before stuffing

➤ During final cooking, stuffing must reach the minimum safe temperature for they food they were stuffed into.

Standard Breading, page 349

Key concepts and terms

chapelure   standard breading procedure   dry bread crumbs
eggwash   bread crumbs
mie de pain   fresh bread crumbs

General Guidelines for Determining Doneness in Meats, Poultry, and Fish, pages 350-51

Temperatures and Descriptions of Degrees of Doneness (table)

Key concepts and terms

à la minute   the way it smells.   carryover cooking
carryover cooking   the way it feels.
USDA's safe cooking   the way it looks.
temperatures   final resting temperatures

Chapter 15 Exercises

Matching

1. Dressing
2. Mie de pain
3. Eggwash

4. Carryover cooking
5. Standard breading procedure
6. Aromatics

_____ a. Herbs, spices, and vegetables used to enhance the flavor and fragrance of food.

_____ b. Stuffing which is baked separately, outside of the meat, poultry, or fish.

_____ c. Fresh bread crumbs.

_____ d. The process of dusting food items in flour, dipping in eggwash, and then coating with breading.

_____ e. A mixture of beaten eggs, egg whites or yolks, and liquid used as a coating.

_____ f. The phenomenon which causes food to continue cooking even after it is removed from the heat source.

Multiple Choice

1. Chapelure is the French term for
   a. standard breading procedure.
   b. dry bread crumbs.
   c. carryover cooking.
   d. stuffing prepared with forcemeat.

2. Which items are generally associated with marinades?
   a. Eggwash, flour, bread crumbs
   b. Mie de pain, acid, aromatics
   c. Oils, chapelure, aromatics
   d. Acids, oils, aromatics

3. The proper sequence for standard breading procedure is
   a. bread crumbs, eggwash, flour.
   b. flour, eggwash, bread crumbs.
   c. eggwash, flour and bread crumbs combined.
   d. flour and bread crumbs combined, eggwash.

4. Stuffing which is baked separately from the main item rather than stuffed inside is known as
   a. forcemeat stuffing.
   b. chapelure.
   c. binding.
   d. dressing.

5. The purpose of the standard breading procedure is
   a. to create a crisp crust on fried food.
   b. to prevent cross-contamination of food items.
   c. to increase the size and bulk of the food.
   d. to add protein.

6. Which of these statements is true about salt and pepper?
   a. Salt and pepper should be applied separately.
   b. It is best to work with a prepared mixture of 3 parts salt to 1 part pepper.
   c. Salt should be applied at the end of cooking time, to reduce the amount of sodium needed.
   d. Salt and pepper are overrated and should be used sparingly, if at all.

True/False

Indicate whether the each of the following statements is true (T) or False (F)

_____ 1. Leftover flour, eggwash, and bread crumbs from standard breading should be refrigerated if they are to be used again.

_____ 2. Tender or delicate foods should not be marinated.

_____ 3. Grains should always be cooked and cooled before being added to stuffings.

_____ 4. Stuffing prepared for roasted birds and baked separately is called dressing.

_____ 5. Seeds and spices should not be toasted on the stovetop, as they tend to burn easily.

_____ 6. Only the yolks of eggs should be used to prepare eggwash.

_____ 7. Grain stuffings can be seasoned, moistened, and bound in a manner similar to bread crumb stuffings.

_____ 8. The purpose of standard breading is to create a crisp crust on fried food.

_____ 9. Items such as cornflakes and coconut may be used in addition to or in place of bread crumbs in the standard breading procedure.

_____ 10. A chef should not rely on touch as a gauge for measuring doneness of meat.

_____ 11. Oils in marinades are used to break down connective fibers to make tough cuts of meat more tender.

Fill in the Blank

1. _____, including wine and vinegar, are used in marinades to change the texture and flavor of foods.

2. _____ refers to the temperature an item reaches which combines cooking temperature with carryover cooking.

3. Seeds and spices are often _____ to enhance their flavor.

4. Herbs, spices, and vegetables used to enhance the flavor and fragrance of food are known as _____.

5. _____ is the French term for fresh bread crumbs. Dry bread crumbs are called _____.

6. Marinating times vary according to a food's texture. _____ foods require less time. _____ foods require more time.

7. Precooked items for stuffing should be cooled to at least _____ before being added to other ingredients. During final cooking, stuffings must reach _____.

8. Ground chicken or turkey should be cooked to _____. Ground beef should be cooked to _____.

9. _____ stuffings usually contain a mixture of chopped or ground meat and other ingredients.

10. Marinades that have been in contact with raw foods may be used as sauces provided they are _____ before using.

11. Cross-contamination of food ingredients can lead to _____.

12. The proper sequence of ingredients for the standard breading procedure is a. _____, b. _____, c. _____.

13. The three senses, that are used to help determine doneness in meats, poultry, and fish, are _____.

14. The proper sequence of ingredients for the standard breading procedure is _____, _____, and _____.

Written/Short Answer

1. Explain the various ingredients for the standard breading procedure and their proper application.

_____

_____

_____

_____

2. What is carryover cooking and what factors might affect it?

_____

_____

_____

_____

3. Why are seeds and spices toasted, and how is it done?

_____

_____

_____

4. What are the ingredients in a simple stuffing? In a more complex stuffing?

_____

_____

_____

_____

5. How is marinating time determined?

_____

_____

_____

_____

CHAPTER **16**

FABRICATING MEATS, POULTRY, AND FISH

Chapter Overview

Meats, poultry, and fish are among the most costly foods purchased in any kitchen. In this chapter, techniques and methods for trimming, tying, and trussing large cuts or whole birds are explained and illustrated, as are techniques associated with a variety of menu cuts and special cuts known as variety meats. Fish and shellfish fabrication techniques include filleting, preparing paupiettes, shucking, peeling, and deveining.

Chapter Objectives

After reading and studying this chapter, you will be able to

➢ Trim fat and silverskin from meats and explain the reasons for doing so.

➢ Cut meats into even portions and shape them so that they will cook evenly.

➢ Cut portion-size steaks and chops from larger cuts as bone-in and boneless cuts.

➢ Prepare certain variety meats.

➢ Tie a roast.

➢ Grind meats properly for quality and safety.

➢ Explain the difference between the two methods covered for preparing a poultry supreme.

➢ Truss poultry for roasting or poaching.

➢ Cut chicken into halves and quarters.

➢ Disjoint a rabbit.

➢ Scale, trim, and gut fish prior to cutting into the desired cut.

➢ Fillet round fish and flat fish, and make a variety of cuts from the fillet.

➢ Handle raw and cooked crustaceans to remove shells and veins.

➢ Clean and shuck oysters, clams, and mussels.

➢ Clean and cut octopus and squid.

Study Outline

Meat Fabrication, pages 358-75

Key concepts and terms

butterfly	frenching	paillard
cutlet	marrow	scallop
eminçé	medallion	steak
fillet/filet	noisette	

Trimming a tenderloin, page 359, illustrations page 359

Shaping a medallion, page 360, illustrations page 360

Fabricating boneless meats, page 361, illustrations page 361 (shows preparation of stew meat and proper set-up with containers for fabricated meat, usable trim, and nonusable trim)

Cutting and pounding cutlets, page 362, illustrations page 362

Shredding and mincing meats, page 362, illustrations page 362

Cutting bone-in chops, page 363, illustrations page 363

Trimming a strip loin and cutting boneless steaks, pages 364-65, illustrations pages 364-65

Trimming and boning a pork loin, page 365, illustrations page 365

Boning a leg of lamb, pages 366-67, illustrations pages 366-67

Frenching a rack of lamb, page 368, illustrations page 368

Working with Variety Meats

Liver, page 369, illustrations page 369

Kidneys, page 369, illustrations page 369

Sweetbreads, page 370, illustrations page 370

Tongue, pages 370-71, illustrations pages 370-71

Marrow, page 371, illustrations page 371

Tying a Roast, pages 372-74, illustrations pages 372-74

Technique one, pages 372-73, illustrations pages 372-73

Technique two, page 374, illustrations page 374

Grinding Meats, page 375, illustrations page 375

➢ Grinding meats calls for scrupulous attention to safe food handling practices.

➢ Cut the meat into dice or strips that will fit easily through the grinder's feed tube.

➢ Chill meats thoroughly before grinding. Chill all grinder parts that will come in contact with the food by either refrigerating them or submerging them in ice water.

➢ Do not force the meat through the feed tube with a tamper. If they are the correct size, the pieces will be drawn easily by the worm.

➢ Be sure that the blade is sharp. Meat should be cut cleanly, never mangled or mashed, as it passes through the grinder.

Poultry Fabrication, pages 376-82

Key Concepts and Terms

disjoint	suprême
keel bone	truss

Preparing a Suprême

Technique one, pages 376-77, illustrations pages 376-77

Technique two, pages 378-79, illustrations pages 378-79

Trussing Poultry, page 380, illustrations page 380

Halving and Quartering Poultry, page 381, illustrations page 381

Disjointing a Rabbit, page 382, illustrations page 359

Fish Fabrication, pages 383-390

Key concepts and terms

cephalopods	goujonette	tranche
fillet	paupiette	viscera

Scaling and Trimming Fish, page 383, illustrations page 383

Gutting a Fish

Round fish, page 384, illustrations page 384

Flat fish, page 384-85, illustrations page 384-85

Cutting fish into steaks, page 385, illustrations page 385

Filleting Fish

Round fish, page 386-87, illustrations page 359 (showing procedure to fillet a whole salmon)

Flat fish, page 388-89, illustrations page 388-89 (showing procedure to make fillets from flounder)

Dover sole, page 389, illustrations page 389

Tranche, page 390, illustration page 390

Goujonette, page 390, illustration page 390

Paupiette, page 390, illustration page 390

Shellfish Fabrication, pages 391-98

Key concepts and terms

beak	devein	tomalley
beard	mantle	
coral	oyster liquor	

Working with Live Lobster, page 391, illustrations page 391

Cooked Lobster, page 392, illustrations page 392

Shrimp, page 393, illustrations page 393

Cleaning and Picking Crayfish, page 394, illustrations page 394

Cleaning Soft-Shelled Crab, page 394-95, illustrations page 394-95

Cleaning and Opening Oysters, Clams, and Mussels

Oysters, page 395, illustrations page 395

Clams, page 396, illustrations page 396

Mussels, page 396, illustrations page 396

Cleaning Squid and Octopus

Octopus, page 397, illustrations page 397

Squid, page 398, illustrations page 398

Chapter 16 Exercises

Matching

1. Trussing
2. Noisettes
3. Viscera
4. Suprême
5. Cutlet
6. Paupiette

7. Butterflying
8. Goujonette
9. Emincé
10. Frenching
11. Keel bone

_____ a.   The cartilage found in the breast of birds.

_____ b.   Meat slices that are cut against the grain into thin strips or slivers.

_____ c.   Removing all meat and fat, scraping bones clean.

_____ d.   A semi-boneless poultry breast half, with wing attached.

_____ e.   A skinless fish fillet, rolled, and usually shallow-poached.

_____ f.   Little "nuts" of meat.

_____ g.   Tying a bird into a neat shape for roasting.

_____ h.   A small, finger-sized piece of fish fillet.

_____ i.   Thin, boneless cut of meat or poultry; also called scallop.

_____ j.   Cutting horizontally through a thick piece of meat to create one that is thinner and has greater surface area.

_____ k.   Another term for the fish's guts.

Multiple Choice

1. The silverskin should be removed before sautéing or grilling foods because it
   a. can shrink, causing the meat to cook unevenly.
   b. tastes bad.
   c. is not kosher.
   d. has an unattractive appearance.

2. Poultry is often purchased whole because
   a. most restaurants roast birds whole, then cut them into pieces.
   b. most poultry is relatively easy to cut into the shape and size needed, and any trim can be used for stocks and other preparations.
   c. that is the only way it is available to restaurants; precut poultry is not readily available.
   d. that is the tradition.

3. Cross-contamination from uncooked poultry can be avoided by making certain to
   a. unwrap and dispose of any plastic or Styrofoam in contact with the birds upon delivery.
   b. store all uncooked birds in the freezer.
   c. clean and sanitize all tools and work surfaces before and after cutting the poultry, and be sure to store them in leakproof containers, below other foods so that they will not drip.
   d. allow only one person in the kitchen to work with raw poultry on a designated cutting board.

4. A suprême of chicken has
   a. two wing joints and some of the rib cage still attached.
   b. no skin and no bones.
   c. skin still on, and a piece of the back still attached.
   d. no skin and no bones, with the exception of one wing joint.

5. The legs of poultry can be separated from the breast by
   a. cutting through the skin and joint just above where the breast and thigh meet.
   b. pulling back the skin and separating with a serrated knife.
   c. ordering them separately.
   d. using a cleaver to cut through the joint.

True/False

Indicate whether the each of the following statements is true (T) or False (F)

_____ 1. Meats are generally cut against the grain for the best texture.

_____ 2. There is more than one way to properly tie a roast.

_____ 3. The technique for a tying a roast with the bone in is very different from that used for a boneless roast.

_____ 4. Butterflying meats is an old-fashioned technique that is rarely used in a contemporary kitchen.

_____ 5. Paillards are always pan-fried or sautéed.

_____ 6. A scallop is one of many terms used to refer to thin, boneless cuts from the loin, leg, or round.

_____ 7. The keel bone is often left attached to the breast when preparing a suprême.

_____ 8. Trussing is a good technique to make certain that birds roast evenly, retain their moisture, and look attractive.

_____ 9. The bones may be left intact for birds that are being grilled to help prevent shrinkage.

_____ 10. It is very important to keep poultry under refrigeration when it is not being worked on.

Fill in the Blank

1. The procedure used to cut a rabbit into pieces is called _____.

2. _____ crabs are a seasonal delicacy in which the shell may be eaten with the meat.

3. _____ and _____ are often served "on the half shell."

4. The layer of membrane covering a leg of lamb is known as the _____.

5. The soft inner substance of bones, often used as a garnish for soups and sauces is called _____.

Written/Short Answer

1. What is the benefit of being able to order larger cuts of meat and fabricate them in-house?

_____

_____

_____

_____

2. Chicken is shown exclusively in the poultry fabrication section. Why is that?

_____

_____

_____

_____

3. Name some of the benefits of buying whole birds. Name several uses for the "trim" and "waste." Why is it important to use this trim and waste?

_____

_____

_____

_____

4. Briefly describe the method for gutting and filleting both flat and round fish.

_____

_____

_____

_____

_____

_____

5. What is the most basic equipment used for fabricating meats?

_____

_____

_____

6. Name and describe several different cuts or menu items that can be prepared from a fillet of fish.

_____

_____

_____

Essays

1. What are the best reasons for learning to properly clean and prepare a wide variety of fish and shellfish?

2. What is the distinction drawn between "menu terms" and retail terms for cuts of meat?

CHAPTER 17

GRILLING AND BROILING, ROASTING AND BAKING

Chapter Overview

Some cooking methods rely on dry heat without fats or oils. The food is cooked either by a direct application of radiant heat (grilling and broiling) or by indirect heat in an oven (roasting and baking). The result of these cooking methods is a highly flavored exterior and a moist interior. Grilling and broiling are quick techniques that are used for naturally tender, portion-size or smaller pieces of meat, poultry, or fish. By contrast, roasting and baking require a longer cooking time and are frequently used with larger cuts of meat, whole birds, and dressed fish.

Chapter Objectives

After reading and studying this chapter, you will be able to

➢ Select and prepare ingredients for grilling and broiling, roasting and baking

➢ Select and prepare equipment for grilling and broiling, roasting and baking, including appropriate service items

➢ Explain what is meant by a "zone" on a grill or broiler and how it can be used to adapt to different foods or different production needs

➢ Clean, preheat, and lubricate a grill or broiler

➢ Grill or broil meats, poultry, and fish to the correct doneness to develop the best flavor and texture in the finished dish

➢ Name the differences between roasting, baking (as it relates to meat, poultry, and fish), poêléing, and spit roasting

➢ Roast or bake meats, poultry and fish to the correct doneness to develop the best flavor and texture in the finished dish

➢ Name the correct procedure for preparing a pan gravy

➢ Carve roasts into portions

Study Outline

Grilling and Broiling

(page 400-04; illustrated on page 402-03; model recipe: Grilled (or Broiled) Sirloin Steak, page 404)

Key Terms and Concepts

broiling	grilling	zones
compound butter	pan grilling	

Basic Method

Select and prepare the ingredients and equipment

How to grill or broil

1. Place the seasoned food on the preheated grill or broiler rods to start cooking and to mark it.

2. Turn the food over and continue cooking to the desired doneness.

3. Evaluate the quality of the finished grilled or broiled food.

Roasting

(pages 405-15; illustrated on pages 408-11; model recipe: Roast Chicken with Pan Gravy, page 415)

Key Terms and Concepts

baking	matignon	smoke-roasting
barding	poêléing	spit-roasting
larding	roasting	

Basic Method

Select and prepare the ingredients and equipment

1. Sear the food (optional). Arrange in a roasting pan, and place in a preheated oven.

2. Arrange in a roasting pan, and place in a preheated oven.

3. Roast, adjusting oven temperature as necessary. Baste as necessary throughout cooking time.

4. Add mirepoix or other aromatic ingredients for a pan sauce or gravy to the roasting pan (optional).

5. Roast foods to the correct doneness and let them rest before serving.

6. Brown the food and clarify the fat.

7. Degrease the pan and prepare the roux.
8. (Optional) Prepare a jus lié.
9. Simmer pan gravy until thickened and well-flavored. Strain.
10. Carve, if necessary and serve with sauce and garnish, if desired.
11. Evaluate the quality of roasted foods.

Barding and Larding

(page 407)

Carving Techniques

(pages 412-14)

     Carving a roast duck

     Carving a rib roast

     Carving a leg of ham in the dining room

     Carving a baked ham in the kitchen

Chapter 17 Exercises

True/False

Indicate whether each of the following statements is True (T) or False (F)

_____ 1.   When roasting or baking, stocks may be used during the cooking process to insure tenderness and moistness.

_____ 2.   The most often used test for doneness in grilled foods is touch.

_____ 3.   The most often used test for doneness in roasted foods is touch.

_____ 4.   When grilling and broiling white meats, they should be cooked through, but not overcooked.

_____ 5.   Poêléing is also known as pan-broiling.

_____ 6.   Grilling is best used for less tender cuts of meat which require high heat.

_____ 7.   When barding an item for roasting, it is best to select a tender cut with lots of marbling.

_____ 8.   Poêléing is a butter-roasting technique which includes a matignon.

_____ 9. Smoke-roasting is best done on an outdoor grill.

_____ 10. Carry-over cooking refers to the fact that foods continue to cook even after they have been removed from the heat source.

Multiple Choice

1. The original form of roasting and the oldest form of cookery is called
    a. pan-roasting.
    b. spit-roasting.
    c. barbecuing.
    d. poêléing.
    e. grilling.

2. A matignon, also called an edible mirepoix, is often used with
    a. poêléing.
    b. barding.
    c. pan-roasting.
    d. pan-broiling.
    e. all of the above.

3. Foods cooked by roasting, grilling, broiling, or poêléing
    a. should be left in large pieces for even cooking.
    b. are always cooked and served rare.
    c. should be naturally tender.
    d. should always have a smoky flavor.
    e. a and c only.

4. Allowing an item to rest after it has roasted
    a. will give the cook time to prepare the rest of the meal.
    b. is an optional technique.
    c. stops the carry-over cooking of the roast.
    d. redistributes the juices that have accumulated in the center of the roast.
    e. none of the above.

5. Larding is the technique of
    a. soaking the meat in a flavorful marinade before cooking.
    b. spearing the meat on a spit to roast over the heat.
    c. covering the meat with thin sheets of fat before roasting.
    d. inserting small strips of fatback into the meat before cooking.
    e. none of the above.

Fill in the Blank

1. A piece of meat should be removed from the oven when the internal temperature is _____ than the desired doneness. It will continue to cook through _____.

2. The most reliable method for determining doneness in roasted items is to use an _____.

3. When poêléing, an edible mirepoix, called _____is often added to the vessel.

4. Stuffing for roasted items should be chilled to at least _____degrees before being combined with the raw food.

5. When grilling, the heat source is located _____the item; when broiling, the heat source is located _____the item.

Matching

_____ 1.	Barbecue	_____ 7.	Pan broiling
_____ 2.	Barding	_____ 8.	Grilling
_____ 3.	Pan gravy	_____ 9.	Poêléing
_____ 4.	Broiling	_____ 10.	Spit-roasting
_____ 5.	Smoke-roasting	_____ 11.	Roasting
_____ 6.	Au jus		

a. A technique used to cook foods where the heat source is located below the food.

b. When roasting, this sauce is the juice released from the roasted item collected in the pan.

c. A technique used in roasting, where the item is wrapped in thin sheets of fatback or caul fat to keep the item moist.

d. A style of grilling, often, a sauce is brushed on the surface of the food near the end of cooking time to give additional flavor, color, and sheen.

e. A technique that cooks foods by surrounding them with dry air in a closed environment.

f. A technique used to cook foods on the top of the stove in a cast iron or other heat-resistant metal pan over intense heat.

g. A type of cooking where the heat source is located above the item to be cooked.

h. Meats allowed to cook in their own juices in a covered vessel on a bed of aromatic vegetables.

i. This technique of roasting involves placing the food on a rod that is turned either manually or with a motor.

j. A type of cooking technique where foods are roasted in a closed vessel along with hardwood chips that have been heated to the point at which they smoke.

k. A sauce used in roasting that is made with a roux that incorporates the fat rendered from the roast.

Written/Short Answer

1. What is carry-over cooking? How can it affect the quality of a roasted item?

   _____

   _____

   _____

   _____

2. List three characteristics of properly grilled foods:

   _____

   _____

   _____

   _____

3. What types of meat are best suited for broiling, roasting, and poêléing? Explain why.

   _____

   _____

   _____

   _____

4. What is smoke-roasting and how is it done?

   _____

   _____

   _____

   _____

5. Describe the procedure for making cross-hatch marks on grilled or broiled foods and why is it done.

   _____

   _____

   _____

   _____

6. What is the purpose of resting roasted items before carving them? What would happen to a roasted item if you carved it without a resting period?

_____

_____

_____

_____

7. What is poêléing and how is it done? What types of meats are best suited for this cooking technique?

_____

_____

_____

_____

Essay

1. Some roasting techniques used today were born out of necessity (smoke-roasting, spit-roasting). Discuss why they were used historically, and why they continue to be popular.

2. Explain special procedures for grilling for banquets and when barbecuing.

CHAPTER 18

SAUTÉING, PAN FRYING, AND DEEP FRYING

Chapter Overview

The cooking techniques presented in this chapter rely on fat or oil as the cooking medium. As the amount of fat is altered from the thin film up to enough to completely submerge foods, different effects are achieved. Sautéing is a technique that cooks food rapidly in a little fat over relatively high heat. The term sauté comes from the French verb *sauter,* or, to jump, and refers to the way foods sizzle and jump in a hot pan. In pan frying, food is cooked more by the oil's heat than by direct contact with the pan. The hot oil seals the food's coated surface and locks the natural juices inside. Pan-fried food is almost always coated—dusted with flour, coated with batter, or breaded. Food is fried in enough oil to cover it by half or two thirds; it is often cooked over less intense heat than in sautéing.

Chapter Objectives

After reading and studying this chapter, you will be able to

➢ describe the differences and similarities between sautéing, stir frying, and searing and determine when each of those techniques is appropriate

➢ select and prepare meats, poultry, or fish for sauteing, pan frying, and deep frying

➢ sauté a variety of foods using the basic method

➢ select and prepare appropriate sauces for sautéed foods directly in the sauté pan

➢ use a safe technique for adding foods to be pan fried to the hot oil in the pan

➢ describe the swimming and basket method for deep frying

➢ determine doneness and evaluate quality in sautéed, pan-fried, and deep-fried foods

Study Outline

Sautéing

Key Terms and Concepts

conditioning the pan	sear
sauté	stir fry

Basic Method

Select and prepare the ingredients and equipment

1. Season the food and dredge or dust with flour if necessary.
2. Preheat the pan and add the cooking fat.
3. Immediately add the food to the pan. Sauté on the first side until browned or golden.
4. Turn the food and continue sautéing to the proper doneness.
5. Remove the food from the pan when it is done and make a sauce with the fond.
6. Finish, garnish, and season the sauce and serve it with the sautéed food.
7. Evaluate the quality of the finished sautéed food.

Pan Frying

Key Terms and Concepts

batter
pan-fry
standard breading

Basic Method

Select and prepare the ingredients and equipment

1. Dry and season the foods for pan frying, and coat as necessary.
2. Heat the fat to the correct temperature.
3. Add the food carefully to the hot fat and pan fry on the first side until a good crust and color are reached.
4. Turn the food once and continue to pan fry until the second side is golden and the food is properly cooked.
5. Drain or blot on clean absorbent paper or cloth. The food is ready to serve now, with a sauce if desired.
6. Evaluate the quality of the finished pan-fried food.

Deep frying

Key Terms and Concepts

basket method	double basket method	swimming method
deep fry	recovery time	tempura

Basic Method

Select and prepare the ingredients and equipment

1. Heat the cooking fat to the proper temperature (generally 325 to 375°F/165 to 190°C)
2. Place the food directly in the fat and cook until done.

Swimming Method

Basket Method

Chapter 18 Exercises

True/False

Indicate whether each of the following statements is True (T) or False (F)

_____ 1. Because the oil helps break down tough fibers in meat, less tender cuts may be used when pan frying.

_____ 2. To avoid cross contamination, only one person should perform the standard breading procedure.

_____ 3. Pan fried foods that are finished in the oven should never be covered.

_____ 4. Only naturally tender foods should be sautéed, and after sautéing, the product should remain tender and moist.

_____ 5. Peanut oil, because of its flavor and high smoking point, is traditionally used for stir-frying.

_____ 6. When deep frying, a rendered fat, such as lard, may be used to create a special flavor.

_____ 7. The object of sautéing is to produce a flavorful exterior, resulting from proper browning.

_____ 8. Stuffed items should never be pan-fried.

_____ 9.   Stir frying is generally associated with Asian styles of cooking.

_____ 10.   Sautéed items are usually coated with batter or bread before cooking.

Multiple Choice

1.   When pan frying, if the finished item is pale and not crisp, it is likely that
     a.   the standard breading was applied incorrectly.
     b.   the oil was too hot.
     c.   the pan was too crowded.
     d.   the breading was stale.

2.   In frying, recovery time refers to
     a.   the length of time it takes the oil to reach the proper temperature before frying.
     b.   the time needed for the oil to regain the proper temperature once the food has been added.
     c.   the amount of time the food will continue to cook after it has been removed from the oil.
     d.   the cooking time of the individual food item.

3.   Kitchens that fry many different foods usually avoid flavor transfer by
     a.   having more than one fryer available.
     b.   straining or filtering the oil after each use.
     c.   frying all of one item before beginning the next.
     d.   blotting the fried foods with absorbent toweling immediately after they are fried.

4.   Searing and sautéing differ because
     a.   searing requires more oil.
     b.   the technique is performed differently.
     c.   seared foods are not cooked completely during searing.
     d.   sautéing is done for portion-sized foods, searing is used for larger cuts.

5.   Sauces served with pan-fried items
     a.   are always made from the fond left in the pan.
     b.   are always made separately.
     c.   are made by deglazing the pan with jus and butter.
     d.   are never used because the item is breaded.

Fill in the Blank

1.   When deep frying, discard the oil if it becomes rancid, smokes below _____
     ____,
     or foams excessively.

2.   When deep frying, the food is almost always coated with _____, _____,
     or _____which acts as a barrier between the food and the fat.

3. _____ indicates that food was sautéed at an overly low temperature or that the pan was too crowded.

4. Stir-frying, generally associated with Asian styles of cooking, shares many similarities with _____.

5. Whereas a sautéed item is lightly dusted with flour and quickly cooked over high heat in a _____ amount of oil, a pan-fried food is usually coated with batter or bread and is cooked in a _____ amount of oil.

Matching

_____ 1. Recovery time	_____ 7. Fond
_____ 2. Pan frying	_____ 8. Deep frying
_____ 3. Sear	_____ 9. Stir frying
_____ 4. Sauté	_____ 10. Swimming method
_____ 5. Tempura	_____ 11. Deglaze
_____ 6. Smoking point	

a. To release the reduced drippings from the bottom of a pan by adding a small amount of liquid and stirring until the drippings lift away.

b. To brown the surface of food in oil or fat over high heat before finishing by another method.

c. The browned drippings which remain in the pan after an item is sautéed.

d. The point at which fats and oils smoke, thus indicating the point at which they break down.

e. A technique, of Asian origin, that cooks bite-size pieces of food quickly in a small amount of very hot oil.

f. A cooking method involving breaded foods cooked in a moderate amount of fat or oil.

g. The technique of cooking food very quickly in a small amount of fat.

h. A deep-frying technique where (usually battered) food is lowered into the oil, and allowed to rise to the surface on its own.

i. A Japanese style of deep frying, in which items are coated with a thin batter that becomes very crisp and lacy as it fries.

j. A technique that cooks foods by submerging them in hot fat or oil.

k. This measures the amount of time it takes the oil to return to the proper temperature after an item is added.

Written/Short Answer

1. What are some of the differences between sautéing and pan frying?

_____

_____

2. What three purposes does a sauce serve with sautéed items?

_____

_____

_____

_____

3. Briefly describe any pre-preparation needed for sautéed food items.

_____

_____

_____

_____

4. Why would you chill a breaded item after it has gone through the standard breading procedure? Why do you not stack foods that have gone through the standard breading procedure? Why is it important to acquire a good seal on the breading when pan frying?

_____

_____

_____

_____

5. Explain the mise en place and preparation of sauces for sautéed items.

_____

_____

_____

_____

6. When deep fat frying, what will happen to food that is added to fat that has not reached the proper temperature?

_____

_____

_____

_____

7. List three possible reasons that fried food might taste heavy, oily, or have the strong flavor of another food.

_____

_____

_____

_____

Essay

1. What are the differences and similarities between sautéing, searing, and stir frying? Explain when and why each technique might be chosen for a specific dish. List a few dishes which are cooked using each technique.

2. Explain the difference in sauces for sautéed, pan-fried, and deep-fried items.

ʏ

CHAPTER **19**

Chapter Overview

Moist-heat techniques—steaming, cooking foods *en papillote*, shallow poaching, deep poaching, and simmering—rely on liquid and/or water vapor as the cooking medium. Monitoring cooking temperatures and times vigilantly and determining doneness accurately are key to a mastery of moist-heat methods.

Cooked surrounded by water vapor in a closed cooking vessel, steamed foods have clean, clear flavors. Steam circulating around the food provides an even, moist environment. En papillote indicates a specific preparation, but there are similar dishes, known by regional names, throughout the world. The classic wrapper for a dish en papillote is parchment paper, but the effect is similar when aluminum foil, lettuce, plantain, grape or banana leaves, corn husks, or similar wrappers are used to enclose foods as they cook.

Shallow-poached foods are partially submerged in liquid. It often contains an acid (wine or lemon juice). Aromatics, such as shallots and herbs, are added for more flavor. The pan is covered to capture some of the steam released by the liquid during cooking; the captured steam cooks the part of the food that is not directly in the liquid.

Deep poaching and simmering are similar techniques. They both that call for a food to be completely submerged in a liquid that is kept at a constant, moderate temperature. The aim of deep poaching and simmering is the same—to produce foods that are moist and extremely tender.

Chapter Objective

After reading and studying this chapter, you will be able to

➢ name and describe each of the following moist-heat techniques —steaming, cooking foods *en papillote*, shallow poaching, deep poaching, and simmering

➢ select and prepare meats, fish, or poultry for each of the moist-heat methods

➢ properly regulate cooking temperatures and determine doneness accurately for each of the moist-heat methods.

➢ use a variety of techniques to add flavor to foods prepared by moist-heat methods

➢ evaluate the quality of foods prepared by moist-heat methods

Study Outline

Steaming

Key Terms and Concepts

convection steamer   steaming
pressure steamer   tiered steamer

Basic Method

Select and prepare the ingredients and equipment

1. Bring the liquid and any additional aromatics to a full boil in a covered vessel.
2. Place the main item in the steamer in a single layer.
3. Replace the lid and steam until done.
4. Steamed foods should be cooked until they are just done and served immediately.
5. Evaluate the quality of the finished dish.

Cooking en Papillote

Key concepts and terms

en papillote
parchment paper
sizzler platter

Basic Method

Select and prepare the ingredients and equipment

1. Assemble the packages.
2. Place the package on a preheated sizzler platter or baking sheet and bake in a moderate oven. Serve immediately.
3. Evaluate the quality of the finished dish.

Shallow Poaching

Key Terms and Concepts

beurre blanc   sauce vin blanc
cuisson   shallow poaching

Basic Method

Select and prepare the ingredients and equipment

1. Butter the pan and add the aromatic ingredients.
2. Add the main item and cooking liquid.
3. Bring the liquid to a bare simmer over direct heat. Loosely cover the pan with parchment paper and finish cooking in a moderate oven.
4. Remove the main item to a holding dish and prepare a sauce from the cooking liquid.
    To make a beurre blanc
    To make a sauce vin blanc
5. Evaluate the quality of the finished shallow-poached item.

Deep Poaching and Simmering

Key Terms and Concepts

boiling
deep poaching
simmering

Basic Method

Select and prepare the ingredients and equipment

1. Combine the food with the liquid and bring to the correct cooking temperature.
2. Maintain the proper cooking speed throughout the poaching or simmering process until the item is done.
3. Poach the food until properly done. Carefully remove it from the liquid.
4. Evaluate the quality of the finished dish.

Chapter 19 Exercises

True/False

Indicate whether each of the following statements is True (T) or False(F)

_____ 1. When deep-poaching, the cooking liquid should always be brought to a boil first before the main item is added.

_____ 2. Foods cooked en papillote may be seared before being wrapped in parchment paper.

_____ 3. When poaching or simmering, a pot that is too large will not produce a flavorful product because the amount of liquid needed to cover the product will be greater.

_____ 4. Covering a pot when cooking has the effect of creating pressure, which allows the liquid's temperature to become lower.

_____ 5. Beurre blanc is a sauce frequently prepared with the cuisson of food cooked en papillote.

_____ 6. Unlike dry-heat methods, moist-heat cookery does not form a seal on the food as an initial step in the cooking process.

_____ 7. When cooking food en papillote, the steam created by the food's natural juices cooks the food.

_____ 8. In shallow poaching, no significant flavor is transferred between the food and the poaching liquid.

_____ 9. Foods cooked en papillote should be cooked until just done.

_____ 10. Foods cooked en papillote can be kept warm in a holding container for a short time without significant lose of quality.

Multiple Choice

1. Poaching and simmering are techniques that call for a food to be
   a. cooked quickly in a small amount of liquid.
   b. partially submerged with liquid.
   c. steamed with aromatic vegetables and herbs.
   d. cooked in a liquid that is kept at a constant, moderate temperature.

2. Poached and steamed items should be
   a. cooked according to the customer's order.
   b. cooked just to the point of doneness.
   c. cooked rare or medium rare.
   d. parcooked, removed from the cooking liquid, and finished in a moderate oven.

3. Items to be steamed should be naturally tender and
   a. of a size or shape that will allow them to cook in a short amount of time.
   b. seared to form a seal on the outside, to prevent moisture and flavor loss during cooking.
   c. free of skin, bones, or shell.
   d. allowed to rest 10-15 minutes before serving for the juices to redistribute in the food item.

4. Foods that have been properly prepared en papillote will demonstrate the same characteristics of flavor, appearance, and texture as
   a. shallow-poached foods.
   b. steamed foods.
   c. simmered foods.

d. poached foods.

5. Fish fillets formed into paupiettes are usually cooked by what technique?
   a. Steaming
   b. Simmering
   c. En papillote
   d. Shallow poaching

Fill in the Blank

1. Deep-poached foods left to cool in their poaching liquid should be _____ to prevent bacterial growth.

2. _____ generally contain a greater proportion of nutrients because water-soluble nutrients are not drawn out of the food as readily.

3. When cooking food en papillote, the main item rests on a bed of herbs, vegetables, or sauce, and the combination of these ingredients and the natural juices serves _____.

4. Like sautéing and grilling, shallow poaching is an _____ technique suited to foods that are cut into portion size or smaller pieces.

5. Poaching and simmering are techniques that call for a food to be completely submerged in a liquid that is kept at a _____ temperature.

Matching

_____ 1. Steamer
_____ 2. Steaming
_____ 3. En papillote
_____ 4. Boiling
_____ 5. Shallow poaching
_____ 6. Simmering
_____ 7. Deep poaching
_____ 8. Parchment
_____ 9. Cuisson
_____ 10. Water vapor
_____ 11. Pressure steamer

a. To cook foods by completely submerging them in liquid at 160°F-185°F/70°C-82°C.

b. The cooking liquid, which might later be used as a base for a sauce.

c. A cooking technique for less tender cuts that cooks them in liquid between 185°F-200°F/82°C-85°C.

d. Steam or steam bath, used as the cooking medium for naturally tender foods.

e. This method cooks foods by surrounding them with a vapor bath.

f. A variation of steaming in which the item is sealed in parchment paper and cooked in a hot oven.

g. A perforated insert or set of stacked pots with perforations that enable food to be cooked in a vapor bath.

h. Food that is partially submerged in liquid and cooked by a combination of steam and simmering liquid.

i. Heat resistant paper used in shallow poaching and for cooking food en papillote.

j. A machine that cooks food using steam produced by heating water in a sealed compartment, allowing it to reach higher than boiling temperature.

k. Vigorous cooking method applied to very few foods because of its potential to cause meats, fish, and poultry to become tough and stringy.

Written/Short Answer

1. What types of food are best suited for steaming? Why might steamed foods generally contain a greater proportion of nutrients?

_____

_____

_____

_____

2. Foods prepared en papillote are baked in a moderate oven. Explain why this cooking technique is considered a moist-heat cooking technique rather than a dry-heat cooking technique.

_____

_____

_____

_____

3. What are some of the difficulties in determining doneness with foods cooked en papillote? How can over-cooking be avoided?

_____

_____

_____

_____

4. List some possible liquids that can be used for steaming and poaching foods.

_____

_____

_____

_____

5. What should be done to simmered or poached foods that are to be served chilled?

_____

_____

_____

_____

6. Why is it important to choose the correct size pot when shallow poaching? When simmering or deep poaching?

_____

_____

_____

_____

7. What effect does covering a pot have in relation to its temperature?

_____

_____

_____

_____

Essay

1. What is the fundamental difference between moist- and dry-heat cooking?

2. What are the similarities in the techniques of shallow and deep poaching? What are the differences?

3. Discuss safe food handling procedures for simmered or poached food that is to be served chilled?

CHAPTER **20**

Chapter Overview

Braises and stews are often thought of as peasant dishes because they frequently call for less tender (and less expensive) main ingredients than other techniques. One of the benefits of these techniques is that tough cuts become tender as the moist heat gently penetrates the meat and causes the connective tissues to soften. Another bonus is that flavor is released into the cooking liquid to become the accompanying sauce; thus, virtually all the flavor and nutrients are retained with a sauce of exceptional body because of the slow cooking needed to break down tough connective tissues. Stews are based on the same cuts of meat, poultry, or fish as a braise. They differ from a braise primarily in the size of the cut; stew meats are typically cut to be mouth-sized pieces while braises are singe, larger cuts that are carved into portions.

Chapter Objectives
After reading and studying this chapter you will be able to

➢ name the similarities and differences between braising and stewing

➢ select and prepare ingredients and equipment for braises and stews

➢ prepare a braise or a stew according to basic guidelines

➢ name a variety of thickening options for stews and braises

➢ finish a stew with a liaison

➢ properly determine doneness in a variety of stews and braises

➢ evaluate the quality of stews and braises

Study Outline

Braises

Key Terms and Concepts

braise	aromatics
cooking liquid	white braise

Basic Method

Select and prepare the ingredients and equipment

Make the braise
1. Prepare the main item for braising and season it.
2. Heat the pan and oil and sear the seasoned main item on all sides to a deep brown.
3. Add the aromatic vegetables to the pan and cook.
4. Add flour to prepare a roux, if desired.
5. Add the appropriate amount of cooking liquid and bring it up to a rapid simmer over direct heat.
6. Add additional ingredients to the braise at the appropriate time so that all elements of the dish are evenly cooked.
7. Braise until the main item is fully cooked and tender.
8. Finish the sauce as necessary. Carve or slice the main item if necessary and serve with sauce and other accompaniments.
9. Evaluate the quality of the finished braise.

Stews

Key Terms and Concepts

blanquette	garnish
stew	liaison

Basic Method

Select and prepare the ingredients and equipment

1. Heat the pan and oil and cook the seasoned main item on all sides or combine the main item with the cooking liquid.
2. Bring the liquid to a simmer over low heat, cover the pot, and finish the stew in a moderate oven or over low direct heat. Stir, skim, and adjust the seasoning and amount of liquid throughout cooking time.
3. Stew the dish until the ingredients are fully cooked and tender to the bite.
4. Add any garnishing ingredients to the stew.
5. Make the final adjustments to the stew's flavor and consistency.
6. Evaluate the quality of the white braise or stew.

Chapter 20 Exercises

True/False

Indicate whether each of the following statements is True (T) or False(F)

_____ 1.   Two benefits of braising are that less tender cuts can be made tender, and that the flavor is captured in braising liquid, which is served with main item.

_____ 2.   Stews differ from braises in that the foods are typically cut into bite-size pieces and are cooked in more liquid.

_____ 3.   In braising, it is necessary to use more seasoning than usual, because the flavor is lost in the braising liquid.

_____ 4.   Acidic ingredients should not be added to braising liquids in the beginning as they will cause the meat, fish, or poultry to tighten.

_____ 5.   In braising, the main item should be seared to a light golden brown, before the cooking liquid is added.

_____ 6.   Cider and cider vinegar are used as ingredients in Yankee Pot Roast to flavor and to tenderize the meat.

_____ 7.   In braising, relatively little liquid is used in relation to the main item's volume.

_____ 8.   Tomatoes, frequently used in braised dishes, act as a tenderizer to break down the tough tissues of less tender meats and give the finished dish additional flavor and color.

_____ 9.   When stewing, searing the meat will assist in developing moisture and texture.

_____ 10.   Braising in the oven tends to result in a inferior product that lends itself to scorching easily.

Multiple Choice

1. In stewing, the amount of liquid used in relation to the amount of item
    a. is always less than braising.
    b. is about the same as braising.
    c. varies from one style of preparation to another.
    d. is more than braising.

2. Tender food items can be braised or stewed, but require
    a. less cooking liquid.

b. a lower temperature.

c. a shorter cooking time.

d. all of the above.

e. none of the above.

3. One similarity in the techniques of braising and stewing is that

a. both require that the main item be completely covered with a cooking liquid.

b. both require that the main item be seared before the cooking liquid is added.

c. both require that the main item be cooked until it is tender enough to cut with a fork.

d. both require that any acidic ingredients should be added at the end of the cooking process, along with any garnishes.

4. After the main item has been seasoned, the next step for most braises is to

a. sear the main item in a small amount of hot fat.

b. blanch the main item in salted water.

c. sweat or caramelize the mirepoix.

d. cut the meat into bite-size portions.

5. Dredging a main item in flour before braising will

a. help the meat to caramelize.

b. help retain the juices inside the meat.

c. help to thicken the sauce during cooking.

d. eliminate the need for trussing.

e. none of the above.

Fill in the Blank

1. Tomatoes are frequently used in braised dishes to _____, _____ and _____. (no particular order)

2. Rather than use flour to thicken a braise, some chefs prefer to add _____ or _____after the braise is complete. (no particular order)

3. When preparing a stew, blanching improves the _____and _____ of the finished product. (no particular order)

4. Preparations that are braised or stewed traditionally have a robust flavor and are often thought of as meals for the _____and _____seasons. (no particular order)

5. Foods to be braised are traditionally _____and _____than foods prepared by dry heat or simmering or steaming. (no particular order)

Matching

_____ 1. Brown braise	_____ 7. Blanquette
_____ 2. Braising	_____ 8. Slurry
_____ 3. White stew	_____ 9. White braise
_____ 4. Roux	_____ 10. Goulash
_____ 5. Bouillabaisse	_____ 11. Ragoût
_____ 6. Stewing	

a. A preparation where the main item is seared only until the exterior stiffens without browning, before the cooking liquid is added.

b. A French term for stew, this literally translates as "restores the appetite."

c. A general term used to describe food that is first seared and then cooked slowly in a liquid medium.

d. A stew originated in Hungary, seasoned and colored with paprika and served with dumplings and potatoes.

e. A Mediterranean-style fish stew, combining a variety of fish and shellfish.

f. A preparation where the main item is seared until deep brown before the cooking liquid is added.

g. A starch (usually cornstarch) mixed with cold liquid; used to thicken hot liquids.

h. A preparation where the main item is added directly to the stewing liquid without being seared.

i. A combination of flour and fat (usually butter) used to thicken liquids.

j. A white stew traditionally made from white meat or lamb, and garnished with mushrooms and pearl onions.

k. A technique similar to braising, where the main item is usually cut into bite-size pieces.

Written/Short Answer

1. Describe the differences between the braising and stewing methods.

_____

_____

_____

_____

2. What types of foods are considered appropriate for combination cooking methods?

_____

_____

_____

_____

3. Why does braising in the oven result in a better product? What precautions should be taken if braising is done on the stovetop?

_____

_____

_____

_____

4. What can be said about the amount of liquid to be used with a stewing compared to braising?

_____

_____

_____

_____

5. Other than searing, what can be done to meat to be stewed in order to improve its flavor and color?

_____

_____

_____

_____

6. What is the purpose of removing the lid during the final portion of the cooking time when braising?

_____

_____

_____

_____

7. What are some thickening options when preparing a braise or stew?

_____

_____

_____

_____

Essay

1. In braising and stewing, what accounts for the sauce's exceptional body?

2. What are 3 possible explanations for an absence of flavor in a braise or stew?

3. Describe how a white braise or stew differs from a brown braise or stew.

CHAPTER 21

MISE EN PLACE FOR VEGETABLES AND FRESH HERBS

Chapter Overview

From trimming and peeling to slicing and dicing, many vegetables and herbs need some kind of advance preparation before they are ready to serve or to use as an ingredient in a cooked dish. Various knife cuts are used to shape vegetables and herbs. A thorough mastery of knife skills includes the ability to prepare vegetables and herbs properly to be cut, to use a variety of cutting tools, and to make cuts that are uniform and precise.

Chapter Objectives

After reading and studying this chapter, you will be able to

➢ explain the importance of proper vegetable cuts to all dishes including vegetables

➢ perform the basic tasks of vegetable preparation using appropriate tools and techniques

➢ name the standard cuts and their appropriate dimensions

➢ cut a variety of vegetables into standard and decorative cuts

➢ master the specific techniques used for specific vegetables and herbs

➢ work with dried fruits and vegetables

➢ describe the general guidelines for vegetable and herb mise en place

Study Outline

Cutting Vegetables And Fresh Herbs

Key Terms and Concepts

allumette	dice	paring knife
battonet	fermière	paysanne
brunoise	julienne	rondelle
chiffonade	lozenge	shredding
chopping	mincing	swivel-bladed peeler
coarse chopping	oblique	tourné

Basic method

Peeling vegetables
Chopping
Mincing
Chiffonade/shredding
Julienne and battonet
Dicing

Making paysanne/fermière cuts
Making diamond/lozenge cuts
Making rounds/rondelles
Making diagonal/bias cuts
Making oblique or roll cuts

Decorative Cuts Using Special Techniques or Tools

Key Terms and Concepts

fanning
fluting

gaufrette
waffle

Basic method

Fanning
Fluting

Waffle/Gaufrette
Cutting turned/tourné vegetables

Preparation Techniques for Specific Vegetables

Key Terms and Concepts

charring
tomato concassé

Basic method

Peeling and cutting onions
Garlic
Roasting garlic
Leeks
Tomatoes
Preparing tomato concassé
Precision cuts for peeled tomatoes
Fresh peppers and chiles
Cutting and seeding fresh peppers and chiles

Peeling fresh peppers or chiles
Mushrooms
Chestnuts
Corn
Artichokes
Pea pods
Avocado
Asparagus

Working With Dried Vegetables and Fruits

Key Terms and Concepts

plumping
rehydrating

Basic method

Rehydrating
Toasting

General guidelines for vegetable and herb mise en place

➢ proper timing

➢ make lists; prioritize

➢ hone knives

➢ wash vegetables and herbs first

➢ arrange work in a logical flow

➢ keep tools and work surfaces clean

➢ sanitize all tools and cutting surfaces when switching from one food to another

➢ wash hands frequently and wear gloves if appropriate

Additional Mise en Place

In addition to the techniques and preparations already discussed, vegetable cookery often requires knowledge of other techniques, many of which can be found elsewhere in this book.

Preparing leafy greens
Toasting spices, nuts, and seeds
Zesting citrus fruit and cutting supremes
Preparing fruits
Marinades
Standard breading procedure

Chapter 21 Exercises

True/False

Indicate whether each of the following statements is True (T) or False(F)

_____ 1. When coarse chopping for mirepoix or vegetables that will be pureed, the vegetable cuts do not need to be uniform in size.

_____ 2. Unlike other minced herbs and vegetables, scallions and chives are minced by slicing very thin.

_____ 3. Electric slicers should never be used to slice vegetables because of the risk of cross contamination with meat products.

_____ 4. To "plump" dried fruits and vegetables, soak them in boiling liquid for several minutes.

_____ 5. Tomatoes should never be sliced on an electric slicer because of the juice.

_____ 6. Roasted and fresh garlic is used interchangeably in recipes.

_____ 7. The choke is the most valued part of the artichoke.

_____ 8. Swivel-bladed peelers and paring knives may be used to peel vegetables and fruit.

_____ 9. Allumette is a cut used primarily for leafy vegetables.

_____ 10. Sprinkling garlic with salt will make it easier to mash.

Multiple Choice

1. Name the particular knife cuts that are used especially for long, cylindrical vegetables, such as parsnips, carrots, and cucumbers.
   a. Rondelle and oblique
   b. Tourné and fanning
   c. Fluting and mincing
   d. Mirepoix and dicing

2. The correct dimension for a paysanne cut is
   a) 1/2" x 1/2" x 1/2"
   b) 3/4" x 3/4" x 3/4"
   c) 1/4" x 1/4" x 1/8"
   d) 1/2" x 1/2" x 1/8"
   e) 1/8" x 1/8" x 2"- 2 1/2"

3. A food item cut into the brunoise will have what dimension ?

   a. six 1/2" sides
   b. 1/8" x 1/8" x 1 to 2"
   c. 1/8" x 1/8" x 1/8"
   d. 1/2" x 1/2" x 1/8"

4. A brunoise is

   a. larger than small dice.
   b. smaller than small dice.
   c. 1/3"x1/3"x1/3".
   d. another name for small dice.
   e. none of the above.

5. Which vegetable cut is often used to stir-fries and other Asian-style dishes?

   a. Oblique
   b. Tourné
   c. Diagonal
   d. Brunoise

Fill in the Blank

1. When _____for mirepoix or vegetables that will be pureed, the vegetable cuts do not need to be perfectly neat, but they should be uniform in size.

2. Dried fruits and vegetables can be plumped or _____by soaking them in boiling liquid for several minutes.

3. Two popular cuts for french fries are (any two)_____.

4. Waffle or gaufrette cuts are made on a _____.

5. _____is a very fine cut made with a chef's knife; used for herbs, garlic, shallots, ginger, and other aromatic ingredients.

Matching

_____ 1. chiffonade

_____ 2. concassé

_____ 3. tourné

_____ 4. paysanne

_____ 5. fluting

_____ 6. dice

a. Vegetables trimmed and shaped to resemble a barrel or football.

b. A decorative cut primarily used on mushrooms

c. A fine, shredded, vegetable cut.

d. A cube shaped cut; brunoise is one example.

e. Peeled, seeded and coarsely chopped.

f. A vegetable cut, in a peasant style, which resembles a square tile.

_____ 1. oblique   _____ 4. gaufrette

_____ 2. lozenge   _____ 5. julienne

_____ 3. milk

a. A long rectangular cut.

b. A diamond-shaped vegetable cut.

c. Roll-cut.

d. A cut made on a mandoline where the finished product resembles a waffle.

e. To score a row of corn kernels then scrape out the flesh and liquid.

Written/Short Answer

1. Give the approximate dimensions for each of the following vegetable cuts: fine julienne, allumette, batonnet, brunoise, small dice, medium dice, large dice, paysanne, rondelle, tourné,

_____

_____

_____

_____

2. Name several decorative cuts and food items with which they are commonly used.

_____

_____

_____

_____

3. Briefly describe the methods for peeling sweet and hot peppers.

_____

_____

_____

_____

4. Describe the process for cleaning a leek.

_____

_____

_____

5. How is tomato concassé prepared?

_____

_____

_____

_____

6. How do you peel and cut an onion?

_____

_____

_____

_____

7. What is chiffonade and how is it done?

_____

_____

_____

_____

Essay

1. Discuss the importance of a well-planned vegetable and herb mise en place.

2. What are some ways to properly peel vegetables? What basic tools are used to peel and cut?

CHAPTER 22

COOKING VEGETABLES

Chapter Overview

Boiling is a fundamental vegetable cooking technique that can result in a wide range of textures, colors, and flavors, depending upon how the technique is applied. Vegetables may be blanched, parcooked (or parboiled), or fully cooked. Steaming shares many similarities with boiling as a cooking technique for vegetables, but steaming cooks through direct contact with steam rather than liquid. Pan-steamed vegetables are prepared in a covered pot with a relatively small amount of liquid and most of the cooking is done by the steam captured in the pan.

The intense heat of grills and broils gives vegetables a rich, bold flavor. Roasted or baked vegetables can be cooked whole or they may be cut to produce a browned exterior. Sauteing and stir frying are used both as the primary cooking technique for vegetables as well as an à la minute finishing technique. Pan frying is similar to sautéing, the main difference being that the amount of oil used is greater than for sautéing. Also, vegetables may be breaded or coated with flour or a batter. When vegetables are deep fried, the results can range from crisp, fragile chips to hearty croquettes with their crisp coating surrounding a moist, flavorful vegetable mixture. Stewed or braised vegetables literally cook in their own juices. The vegetables in a stew are customarily cut into small pieces, while those in a braise are in large pieces or are left whole.

Chapter Objectives
After reading and studying this chapter, you will be able to

➢ describe a variety of techniques for cooking vegetables

➢ evaluate cooked vegetables according to the appropriate quality standards according to technique

➢ explain how to prepare vegetables in advance to improve efficiency during service periods

➢ select and prepare ingredients and equipment for a variety of cooking methods

➢ determine doneness in vegetables according to the appropriate quality standards

Study Outline

Boiling

Key Terms and Concepts

blanch
boil
parboil

Basic method

Select and prepare the ingredients and equipment

1. Season the cooking liquid and bring it to the proper cooking temperature before adding the prepared vegetables.
2. Cook the vegetables to the desired doneness. Drain thoroughly in a colander or sieve.
3. Evaluate the quality of the finished boiled vegetable.

Determining Doneness in vegetables

Blanched: Vegetables are immersed briefly, usually 30 seconds to 1 minute, depending on ripeness, in boiling water to make the skin easy to remove, to eliminate or reduce strong odors or flavors, to set the color of vegetables to be served cold, and/or as the first step in other cooking techniques.

Parcooked/parboiled: Vegetables are cooked to partial doneness, to prepare them to be finished by grilling, sautéing, or stewing

Tender-crisp or al dente: Vegetables are cooked until they can be bitten into easily, but still offer a slight resistance and sense of texture. (The term al dente, which is Italian for to the tooth, is more accurately used to describe the desired doneness of pasta rather than vegetables.)

Fully cooked: Vegetables are quite tender, though they should still retain their shape and color. If boiling vegetables to make a purée, boil them until they almost fall apart on their own.

Steaming

Key Terms and Concepts

convection steamer
pressure steamer
steaming
tiered steamer

Basic method

Select and prepare the ingredients and equipment

1. Bring the liquid to a full boil in the bottom of a covered steamer. Add the vegetable to the steamer in a single layer.
2. Replace the cover, and steam the vegetable to the desired doneness.
3. Evaluate the quality of the finished steamed vegetable.

Pan Steaming

Key Terms and Concepts

glaze
pan steaming

Basic method

Select and prepare the ingredients and equipment

1. Bring the cooking liquid to a simmer and season or flavor it as desired.
2. If desired, sweat or smother the vegetables and any aromatics in a cooking fat or in the cooking liquid.
3. Pour or ladle enough cooking liquid into the pan to properly cook the vegetables. Cover the pan and cook until the vegetables are done.
4. Cover the pan and cook until the vegetable is done.
5. If desired, remove the cover and let the cooking liquid continue to reduce to make a glaze or a pan sauce.
6. Evaluate the quality of the pan-steamed vegetable.

Grilling and Broiling

Key Terms and Concepts

broil
grill

Basic method

Select and prepare the ingredients and equipment

1. Place the prepared vegetable directly on the grill or broiler rods. Vegetables can be seasoned with a marinade prior to grilling or broiling.
2. Grill or broil the vegetables, turning as necessary, until properly cooked.
3. Evaluate the quality of the finished grilled or broiled vegetable.

Roasting and Baking

Key Terms and Concepts

bake
purée
roast

Basic method

Select and prepare the ingredients and equipment

1. Prepare vegetables for roasting, as appropriate, by type or intended use and arrange in a baking or roasting pan.
2. Place the prepared vegetable in a hot or moderate oven and roast to the desired doneness. Serve immediately, hold for later use, or use as an ingredient in another dish.
3. Evaluate the quality of the finished roasted or baked vegetables.

Puréeing

1. vegetables boiled, steamed or baked until soft enough to puree
2. some naturally soft enough to puree from raw state
3. remove rinds, stems, or roots
4. scoop or squeeze out seeds
5. remove as little edible flesh as possible
6. use food mill, ricer, sieve to remove fibers, skin, and seeds
7. food processor to make smooth purees (may require sieving to remove fibers)
8. use puree according to need
9. cool and store properly for later use

Sautéing and Stir Frying

Key Terms and Concepts

sauté
stir fry

Basic method

Select and prepare the ingredients and equipment

How to sauté or stir fry vegetables
1. Heat the oil or fat and add any aromatic ingredients, as desired.
2. Add the prepared vegetable to the pan.
3. Add seasonings and continue to sauté or stir fry until the vegetables are fully cooked and flavorful.
4. Evaluate the quality of the finished sautéed or stir-fried vegetable.

Finishing and glazing vegetables by sautéing

Pan Frying

Key Terms and Concepts

pan fry   standard breading
finishing ingredients   batter

Basic method

Select and prepare the ingredients and equipment

1. Heat the cooking fat in a heavy-gauge skillet, rondeau, or brazier. Add the vegetable carefully.
2. Cook the vegetable over moderate to high heat until the first side becomes lightly browned and crisp. Turn the vegetable and complete the cooking on the second side.
3. Evaluate the quality of the finished pan-fried vegetable.

Deep Frying

Key Terms and Concepts

croquette
deep fry

Basic method

Select and prepare the ingredients and equipment

1. Heat the oil in a deep fryer or kettle. Add the vegetables to the hot oil using a basket, tongs, or a spider.
2. Fry the vegetables until fully cooked. Remove and drain. Season if necessary.
3. Evaluate the quality of the finished deep-fried vegetable.

Stewing and Braising

Key concepts and terms

braise
stew

Basic method

Select and prepare the ingredients and equipment

How to stew or braise vegetables
1. Cook the aromatic vegetables in a cooking fat, beginning with members of the onion family.
2. Add the remaining ingredients in order, stirring as necessary and adjusting the seasoning and consistency of the dish as it braises or stews.
3. Stew or braise the vegetable until it is flavorful, fully cooked, and fork tender. Serve immediately or hold for later use.

    Finishing Options
    The stew or braise is ready to serve now, but it may be finished by preparing a sauce from the cooking liquid. To do so, remove the vegetable from the cooking liquid and thicken the liquid in one of the following ways:
    reduce the liquid to a sauce-like consistency and adjust the seasoning with salt and pepper
    purée some of the aromatic vegetables and return the purée to the cooking liquid
    add a starch slurry
    add a bit of beurre manié to the cooking liquid
4. Evaluate the quality of the finished stewed or braised vegetable.

Chapter 22 Exercises

True/False

Indicate whether each of the following statements is True (T) or False(F)

_____ 1. All vegetables can be sautéed successfully from their raw state.

_____ 2. When sautéing, vegetables can be partially cooked or in their raw state.

_____ 3. Leafy greens should not be sautéed as they loose too much volume during the cooking process.

_____ 4. With the exception of potatoes, when boiling vegetables, they should be added to water that has been brought to a rolling boil.

_____ 5. Covering a pot when cooking has the effect of creating pressure, which prevents the liquid's temperature from reaching the boiling point.

_____ 6. Vegetables in a stew are customarily cut into small pieces, whereas those in a braise are cut in large pieces or are left whole.

_____ 7. Blanching vegetables helps to eliminate strong odors and flavors.

_____ 8. Braising vegetables helps to eliminate strong odors and flavors.

_____ 9. The correct doneness of a vegetable will depend in part upon the style of a particular cuisine or regionally preference.

_____ 10. Some vegetables may be sautéed from the raw state, especially those that are naturally high in moisture.

Multiple Choice

1. A classic ratatouille is an example of which cooking technique?
   a. Roasting
   b. Stewing
   c. Steaming
   d. Au gratin

2. Generally speaking, the best color is retained when vegetables

a. has salt added to the water.
b. are started in cold water.
c. are cooked for as short of time as possible.
d. stored in water.
e. any of the above.

3. In order to correctly determine vegetables doneness a chef should be able to understand
   a. the cost of the vegetable.
   b. the normal standard of quality for a particular cooking technique.
   c. regional and cultural preferences regarding doneness.
   d. the natural characteristics of the vegetable.

4. Vegetable stews and braises are excellent ways to retain vitamins and minerals lost from the vegetable into the cooking liquid because
   a. the liquid is served as part of the dish.
   b. the vegetables are seared first to keep in the vitamins and minerals, along with flavor and juices.
   c. the vegetables are blanched in an acid in the beginning of the cooking process, which helps retain vitamins and minerals.
   d. vegetables are cooked over slow, even heat, which helps retain the vitamins and minerals.

5. To retain the color when boiling red and white vegetables, you should always
   a. add a touch of baking soda.
   b. cover the pot.
   c. start in cold water.
   d. keep the peels on.

Fill in the Blank

1. Stir-frying, generally associated with Asian styles of cooking, shares many similarities with

   _____.

2. When deep frying, the amount of time it takes the oil to return to the proper temperature after the vegetable is added is called the _____.

3. The Japanese style of deep-frying, _____, uses a thin batter which becomes crisp and light when fried.

4. The best temperature for deep frying most vegetables is about _____ ____degrees.

5. Three preferred methods for reheating vegetables are _____, _____

   ____,
   or _____.

Written/Short Answer

1. Explain some possible types of liquids that can be used for boiling, steaming, and pan steaming foods.

    _____

    _____

    _____

    _____

2. What is pan steaming, and how is it done? How does it vary to according to the type of vegetables? How can it vary to influence flavor of the vegetables?

    _____

    _____

    _____

    _____

3. What are three methods of properly reheating vegetables for service?

    _____

    _____

    _____

    _____

4. Why are some vegetables sautéed from their raw state, while others are partially cooked?

    _____

    _____

    _____

    _____

5. What is glazing, and what ingredients are used? What is the method?

    _____

    _____

    _____

    _____

6. What is blanching? List three reasons for blanching foods. Give an example for each reason.

_____

_____

_____

_____

7. How can vegetables be prepped for pan frying and deep frying? Why are few vegetables fried from their raw state?

_____

_____

_____

_____

Essay

1. In order to determine doneness of vegetables, what must the chef understand? When determining doneness of vegetables, what qualities are evaluated and how are they evaluated?

2. What are guidelines to follow when purchasing, cooking, and holding vegetables to assure that they will have the best color, most flavor, and greatest degree of nutrient retention?

3. What is the technique of puréeing vegetables? What equipment can be used to purée? How are puréed vegetables served?

CHAPTER 23

COOKING POTATOES

Chapter Overview

Potato varieties differ in starch and moisture content, skin and flesh color, and shape. Sweet potatoes and yams, although not botanically related to the potato, share several characteristics with it and can be treated in the same manner. Each technique produces a markedly different texture, flavor, and appearance. In addition, different potato varieties will produce different results. Knowing the natural characteristics of each kind of potato and the ways in which a particular technique can either enhance or detract from these characteristics is important to any chef.

Chapter Objectives

After reading and studying this chapter, you will be able to

➢ name the three basic categories of potatoes and explain how moisture and starch content affects the characteristics of the potato after cooking

➢ distinguish potato varieties according to their starch and moisture content and list appropriate preparations made from them

➢ select and prepare potatoes, other ingredients, and equipment for a variety of cooking methods: boiling, steaming, pureeing, baking en casserole, baking and roasting, sautéing, and deep frying

➢ name a variety of familiar potato dishes and the cooking method used to prepare them

➢ prepare potatoes according to the standard methods

➢ determine proper doneness in potatoes and evaluate potato dishes for quality according to the appropriate standards

Potato varieties

Low moisture/high starch
Moderate moisture and starch
High moisture/low starch

Study Outline

Boiling Potatoes

Key Terms and Concepts

boiling	russets	steaming
en chemise	solanine	waxy yellow

Basic method

Select and prepare the ingredients and equipment

1. Place the potatoes in a pot of an appropriate size and cover completely with cold water. Add salt and/or other seasonings as necessary to the cooking liquid.
2. Bring to a boil and cook at a simmer or low boil until the potatoes are done.
3. Evaluate the quality of the finished boiled potatoes.

Steaming potatoes

➢ alternative to boiling

➢ arrange in even layers on racks or inserts

➢ use convection or pressure steamers for large quantities

➢ the larger the potato, the longer the steaming time

➢ add various herbs, spices, or aromatics to the cooking liquid or scatter directly on potatoes during steaming

Puréeing

Key Terms and Concepts

pomme duchesse	potato croquettes
pommes lorette	puréeing

Basic method

Select and prepare the ingredients and equipment

How to purée potatoes
1. Cook the potatoes until very tender by boiling, steaming, or baking. Warm the milk or cream.
2. Push hot drained and dried potatoes through a warmed food mill or ricer. For best results, the potatoes must be hot and the equipment heated.
3. Add seasonings and any additional ingredients, as desired or according to the recipe.

4. Pipe or spoon the potatoes into the desired shape.
5. Evaluate the quality of the finished pureed potatoes.

Baking and Roasting Potatoes

Key Terms and Concepts

baking
roasting

Basic method

Select and prepare the ingredients and equipment

1. Prepare the potatoes for roasting.
2. Season the potatoes, pierce, and bake or roast the potatoes until tender.
3. Evaluate the quality of the finished baked or roasted potato.

Baking Potatoes En Casserole

Key Terms and Concepts

au gratin	dauphinoise	scalloped potatoes
baking	en casserole	

Basic method

Select and prepare the ingredients and equipment

1. Slice low-moisture or waxy yellow potatoes. Par-cook in the liquid called for in the recipe, if desired.
2. Layer the potatoes in the greased pan or pans with the cooking liquid. Arrange raw or par-cooked potatoes in single layers, separating the slices so they will cook evenly.
3. Add topping ingredients at the appropriate time to create a crust.
4. Bake in a moderate (300 to 325°F/150 to 165°C) oven until the potatoes are just tender and the top is golden brown.
5. Evaluate the quality of the finished potatoes en casserole.

Sautéing potatoes

Key Terms and Concepts

Anna potatoes	home fries	rösti
hashbrowns	Lyonnaise	sautéing

Basic method

Select and prepare the ingredients and equipment

1. Prepare the potatoes for sautéing, as appropriate.
2. Heat the fat in an appropriately sized pan. Add the potatoes to the hot fat and sauté until tender.
3. Evaluate the quality of the finished sautéed potatoes.

Deep Frying Potatoes

Key Terms and Concepts

blanch	matchstick	waffle cut
deep frying	soufflé	
french fries	steak fries	

Basic method

Select and prepare the ingredients and equipment

1. Scrub, peel, cut, and rinse the potatoes for deep frying. Blanch them in hot oil.
2. Deep fry the potatoes at 350 to 375°F/176 to 190°C until done.
3. Evaluate the quality of the finished deep-fried potatoes.

Chapter 23 Exercises

True/False

Indicate whether each of the following statements is True (T) or False (F)

_____ 1. To prevent discoloration of raw potatoes, submerge them in acidulated water until time to cook.

_____ 2. When preparing potatoes en casserole, a very creamy texture can be achieved by cooking the dish in a microwave on a low, even temperature. This will also prevent the custard from curdling.

_____ 3. The higher the starch content in a potato, the more granular and dry it will be after it is cooked.

_____ 4. When sautéing potatoes, they should be dried carefully to prevent the oil from splattering.

_____ 5. When boiling potatoes, salt should be added at the end of the cooking time, or it will cause the skins to tighten and slow down the cooking process.

_____ 6. Wrapping a potato in foil before baking will cause it to steam rather than bake.

_____ 7. Potatoes should be pierced before baking, or they might burst.

_____ 8. Sautéed potatoes can be held up to one hour in a steam table before losing quality.

_____ 9. When sautéing potatoes, salt added at the beginning of the cooking process will prevent the potatoes from cooking evenly.

_____ 10. When preparing matchstick potatoes, the potatoes should be parcooked before frying, to prevent them from clumping.

Multiple Choice

1. Which prepared potato would be best suited for long holding periods?
   a. Baked potatoes
   b. Parslied new potatoes
   c. En casserole
   d. French-fried potatoes

2. A potato that is to be puréed must first be
   a. cooked until very tender.
   b. blanched in hot oil.
   c. sautéed in butter or oil.
   d. combined with eggs or pâte à choux.

3. In order for potatoes to retain most of their nutrients, they should be
   a. cooked in their skins.
   b. blanched to "set" the vitamins in the potato.
   c. low moisture and high starch.
   d. cooked using only a single stage technique.

4. A variation of roasted/baked potatoes that calls for the potato to be browned and glazed with oil, butter, or the released drippings from a roast is called
   a. rösti potatoes.
   b. oven-roasted.
   c. twice-baked potatoes.
   d. home fries.
   e. potatoes Anna.

172

5. When sautéing potatoes, the potatoes that give the best texture and appearance to the finished dish are
   a. low-moisture/low-starch potatoes.
   b. low-moisture/high-starch potatoes.
   c. moderate-moisture/moderate-starch potatoes.
   d. high-moisture/low-starch potatoes.

Fill in the Blank

1. When preparing matchstick potatoes, the potatoes should be _____ before frying, to prevent them from clumping.

2. _____ is a technique where the potato is peeled, combined with heavy cream, a sauce, or uncooked custard, and slowly baked until it is extremely tender.

3. Deep-fried potatoes, such as (name 2)_____ are made from a puréed appareil.

4. When deep-frying potatoes in two stages, they are first blanched at _____ and then finished in oil heated to _____.

5. Souffléd potatoes must be blanched before frying to make sure they _____ ____adequately.

Matching

_____ 1. duchesse   _____ 4. purée

_____ 2. matchstick   _____ 5. au gratin

_____ 3. blanch   _____ 6. Anna

a. potatoes, raw or parcooked, combined with a liquid, topped with cheese and/or bread crumbs, and baked in the oven.

b. sliced potatoes, sautéed in a great deal of butter.

c. fully-cooked potatoes which are mashed or processed to be served on their own, or finished using another cooking technique.

d. parcooking potatoes in hot oil before deep frying to finish cooking at service time.

e. cut for deep-fried potatoes, allumette.

f. puréed potato piped onto a sheet pan and baked.

_____ 1. en casserole   _____ 4. Lyonnaise

_____ 2. waffle-cut   _____ 5. en chemise

_____ 3. solanine

a. thick sliced (or diced) parcooked potatoes which are sautéed with onions.

b. toxic in potatoes, its presence indicated by green spots on the potato.

c. in the skin, refers to unpeeled potatoes

d. potatoes, raw or parcooked, combined with a liquid and flavoring ingredients and baked in the oven.

e. vegetable cut made on a mandoline, used for deep fried potatoes.

Written/Short Answer

1. If you store peeled potatoes in water, why is it a good idea to cook the potatoes in that same water?

_____

_____

_____

_____

2. How do you blanch potatoes, what is its purpose, and when is it used?

_____

_____

_____

_____

3. Briefly describe the procedure for puréeing potatoes. Why should you not use a food processor or blender when puréeing potatoes?

_____

_____

_____

_____

4. What are oven-roasted potatoes? What type of potatoes are best suited for this technique?

_____

_____

_____

_____

5. Describe the method for potatoes cooked en casserole.

_____

_____

_____

_____

6. Briefly describe the method for sautéing potatoes. Give the guidelines for determining doneness, and evaluating quality for sautéed potatoes. What variety of cooking fats can be used to sauté?

_____

_____

_____

_____

7. Briefly describe the procedure for deep frying potatoes. What potatoes are best suited for this cooking method?

_____

_____

_____

_____

Essay

1. What would be the advantages of serving potatoes en casserole for banquet service, or restaurant service?

2. Explain the natural characteristics of potatoes regarding moisture and starch content. Give examples of each type of potato and possible cooking methods.

3. Why does a chef need to understand the characteristics of the potato?

CHAPTER 24

Cooking Grains and Legumes

Chapter Overview

Legumes, or beans, are seeds that grow in pods. These seeds can be used in the kitchen fresh or dried. When fresh, they are considered vegetables. Dried, they are known collectively as legumes. Lima beans, for example, are a vegetable when fresh and a legume when dried. Legumes are a potent nutrient source, and they have an even higher protein content than most grains.

Grains are the fruit and seed of cereal grasses. For the most part, they are inexpensive and readily available and provide a valuable and concentrated source of nutrients and fiber. Although grains differ in appearance from other fruits (apples and pears, for example) their botanical composition is quite similar.

Although grains (whole grains, meals, and cereals) legumes are often referred to as boiled, they are actually simmered or steamed. The high heat of a boiling liquid tends to toughen them. When the liquid is completely absorbed by a grain as it cooks, it is often referred to as steamed. Pilaf (also called *pilau*) is a grain dish in which the grain—usually rice—is first heated in a pan, either dry or in fat, and then combined with a hot liquid and cooked, covered, over direct heat or in the oven. In the Italian rice dish risotto, the rice is parched as in the pilaf method, but the liquid is added and absorbed gradually while the grain is stirred almost constantly. The starch is slowly released during the cooking process, producing a creamy texture.

Chapter Objectives

After reading and studying this chapter, you will be able to

➤ select the proper advance preparation method for a variety of grains and legumes

➤ name the two basic approaches to soaking legumes and discuss the pros and cons of soaking versus not soaking legumes

➤ select and prepare grains (whole, cereals, and meals) and legumes, other ingredients, and equipment for a variety of cooking methods: boiling (simmering), steaming, pilaf, and risotto

➤ name a variety of familiar grain and legume dishes and the cooking method used to prepare them

➤ prepare grains (whole, cereals, and meals) and legumes according to the standard methods

➤ determine proper doneness in grains (whole, cereals, and meals) and legumes and evaluate dishes for quality according to the appropriate standards

Study Outline

Simmering Whole Grains and Legumes

Key Terms and Concepts

grains

legumes

long soak method

quick soak method

rehydrate

simmering

Basic method

Select and prepare the ingredients and equipment

The long soak method:
- sort and rinse beans
- place in cool water to cover
- soak under refrigeration for 4 hours or up to 12 hours (see chart on page xxx)
- drain and rinse before continuing

The quick soak method:
- sort and rinse beans
- place in a pot in cool water to cover
- bring to a simmer
- remove pot from heat and cover
- steep legumes in hot water for 1 hour
- drain and rinse before continuing

1. Combine the grain or legume with the cooking liquid and bring to a full boil.
2. Reduce the heat slightly to a simmer and cook the grain or legume until done as desired.
3. Drain the grain or legume or let it cool in the cooking liquid. Finish and serve on heated plates or use in another preparation.
4. Evaluate the quality of the finished boiled legume or whole grain.

Simmering and Boiling Cereals and Meals

Key Terms and Concepts

boiling

bran

cereal

coarse ground

fine ground

germ

meals

milling

simmering

steep

Basic method

Select and prepare the ingredients and equipment

1. Depending on the grain, bring the liquid to a full boil and add the cereal or meal in a thin stream, stirring constantly or combine the cereal and liquid and bring to a boil.
2. Reduce the heat to establish a simmer and cook, stirring as necessary, until done.
3. Evaluate the quality of the finished cooked meal or cereal.

Pilaf

Key Terms and Concepts

parch
pilaf
pilau

Basic method

Select and prepare the ingredients and equipment

1. Sweat the aromatic vegetables in fat or oil until softened. Add the grains and sauté, stirring frequently, until they are well coated with fat.
2. Heat the liquid, add it to the grain, and bring to a simmer. Cover the pot and complete the cooking in a moderate oven or over low heat on the stovetop.
3. Evaluate the quality of the finished pilaf.

Risotto

Key Terms and Concepts

all'onda   risotto
Arborio   parch

Basic method

Select and prepare the ingredients and equipment

1. Sweat the aromatic ingredients in fat until translucent. Add the rice and parch it until well coated.
2. Add the simmering liquid in parts.
3. Stir constantly as the rice cooks.
4. Add the finishing ingredients.
5. Evaluate the quality of the finished risotto.

Chapter 24 Exercises

True/False

Indicate whether each of the following statements is True (T) of False (F)

_____ 1. Cooked legumes may be held for several days without losing quality if properly stored and reheated.

_____ 2. When preparing a pilaf, heating the grain in hot fat or oil begins to gelatinize the starches. This encourages the grains to remain separate after they are cooked.

_____ 3. If wine is to be used when making a risotto, it always should be added at the beginning of the cooking process.

_____ 4. Adding acidic ingredients (tomatoes, vinegar, citrus juice, wine) will tend to slow the softening of grains and legumes.

_____ 5. When grain meals are properly boiled (e.g., as polenta) they will pull cleanly away from the sides of the pot.

_____ 6. Pilafs may be prepared with grains other than rice.

_____ 7. Risotto is traditionally made with a special type of medium-grain rice, known as Arborio.

_____ 8. With a few notable exceptions (lentils, split peas, and black-eyed peas), all legumes must be soaked before cooking.

_____ 9. Couscous is a grain that is steeped rather than boiled.

_____ 10. Boiled grains are less tender and fluffy than those prepared by the pilaf method.

Multiple Choice

1. The type of rice typically used for risotto is
    a. Basmati.
    b. Carolina.
    c. Arborio.
    d. Jasmine.

2. Which of the following best describes the consistency of properly prepared risotto?
    a. Porridge-like

b. Smooth
c. Thin
d. Fluffy

3. The proper cooking sequence for polenta is
   a. boil the liquid, season with salt, add the cornmeal in a stream, cook until firm enough to cut into shapes.
   b. combine the liquid, salt, and cornmeal and bring to a boil, cook until firm enough to cut into shapes.
   c. combine the liquid, salt, and cornmeal and bring to a boil, simmer until thick and smooth.
   d. boil the liquid, season with salt, add the cornmeal in a stream, simmer until thick and smooth.

4. The proper cooking sequence for rice pilaf is
   a. boil the liquid and salt, sweat the aromatics, add the parched rice in a stream; simmer until all liquid is absorbed.
   b. sweat the aromatics, combine hot liquid, rice, and salt, and simmer until all liquid is absorbed.
   c. combine the hot liquid, rice, and salt and bring to a boil; simmer until thick and smooth.
   d. sweat the aromatics, parch the rice, add hot liquid and cook until all liquid is absorbed.

5. Soaking is not essential in the advance preparation in grains and legumes, although it
   a. is always necessary when making a pilaf.
   b. is usually done with grains but not legumes.
   c. is helpful in shortening the cooking time.
   d. is recommended to help retain nutrients in grains and legumes.

Fill in the Blank

1. Grains are often cooked in an amount of liquid that is _____ what they will absorb. Cereals and meals are generally cooked in an amount of liquid that is _____ what they will absorb.

2. _____ legumes will help shorten the cooking time.

3. Polenta is dish made with coarse _____.

4. In general, salt needs to be added at _____ of the cooking time for grains, and _____ of the cooking time for legumes.

5. When cooking legumes, the three things that determine the amount of liquid required are _____, _____, and _____.

Matching

_____ 1. pilaf   _____ 4. cereal
_____ 2. polenta   _____ 5. all'onda
_____ 3. bran   _____ 6. risotto

a. An Italian dish, a combination of coarse ground cornmeal, butter, water, and salt that is slowly simmered.

b. A method of cooking medium-grain round rice by stirring constantly as stock is added a small amount at a time and is absorbed by the grain.

c. wavelike, the Italian term to describe properly cooked risotto.

d. the outer layer of grains.

e. A grain dish in which the grain is first heated in the pan, either dry or in oil, and then combined with hot liquid.

f. A ground grain, such as buckwheat groats, cooked in simmering water or stock until it has thickened, but is liquid enough to pour while still warm.

_____ 1. parch   _____ 4. steep
_____ 2. mill   _____ 5. Arborio
_____ 3. meal

a. The process of soaking in boiling water, grains are soaked in order to soften them enough to be easily chewed.

b. A type of Italian medium-grain round rice used for making risotto.

c. The grinding or breaking down of whole grains into cracked or ground particles.

d. Heating a grain in a hot pan with or without oil.

e. A ground grain, such as grits, cooked in simmering water or stock until it has thickened, but is liquid enough to pour while still warm.

Written/Short Answer

1. How and why should beans and legumes be sorted and rinsed?

_____

_____

_____

_____

2. What is the purpose of soaking legumes? List and describe the two methods used to soak legumes.

_____

_____

_____

_____

3. What effect do acidic ingredients have during the cooking process of grains and legumes? When should they be added during cooking?

_____

_____

_____

_____

4. Briefly describe the guidelines for determining doneness and evaluating quality in grains and legumes that have been boiled.

_____

_____

_____

_____

5. When making a pilaf, what effect does heating the grain in hot oil or fat have on the final product?

_____

_____

_____

_____

6. What are the guidelines for determining doneness and evaluating quality in a risotto? What accounts for a risotto's creamy texture when properly cooked?

_____

_____

_____

_____

7. What advance preparation can be done to risotto in order to serve it throughout a service period without losing quality?

_____

_____

_____

8. Name some dried legumes that are not soaked before cooking.

_____

_____

_____

_____

Essay

1. Describe the proper procedure for preparing risotto. Identify the type of rice used.

2. How is pilaf prepared? What types of cooking liquids can be used with a pilaf?

3. What is polenta? What are the serving options?

CHAPTER 25

Cooking Pasta and Dumplings

Chapter Overview

The immense popularity of pastas and dumplings is not at all surprising. Nutritious and highly versatile, these foods are an important element of most cuisines. They are based on ingredients that are inexpensive and easy to store: flours, meals, and eggs. They adapt well to a number of uses and can be found on contemporary menus as appetizers, entrées, salads, and even desserts.

Dried and fresh noodles are both included in the general category of pasta. Pasta may be prepared fresh on the premises or purchased as either fresh or dried. There are advantages to both fresh and dried pastas. Fresh pasta gives the chef freedom to create dishes with special flavors, colors, or shapes, or fillings, but it has a limited shelf life. Dried pasta can be stored almost indefinitely.

Although the term dumpling may mean something very specific to an individual or a particular ethnic group, it actually is a very broad category. Some dumplings are based on doughs and batters, others on ingredients ranging from bread to pureed potatoes. The popular Chinese dim sum, including steamed yeast doughs and fried egg rolls, is yet another category. Dumplings may be cooked in a variety of ways, according to type. They may be simmered in liquid, steamed, poached, baked, pan-fried, or deep-fried. A variety of ingredients can be used, depending on what sort of dumpling is being prepared. See the recipes included in this chapter for specific instructions.

Chapter Objectives

After reading and studying this chapter, you will be able to

> identify key similarities and differences between fresh and dried pastas

> select and prepare ingredients and equipment for preparing fresh pasta

> cook fresh and dried pastas to the correct doneness

> name the correct procedures for preparing pastas in advance

> roll and cut fresh pasta by hand or using a machine

> use the general guidelines on fresh and dried pastas for serving and reheating

Study Outline

Making Fresh Pasta, Noodles, and Dumplings

Key Terms and Concepts

base recipe	extrusion pasta maker	fettucini
batter	formula	linguini
dough	fresh pasta	ravioli
dough hook	pasta rolling machine	tortellini
dried pasta	semolina	macaroni
dumpling	spätzle	ziti

Basic method

Select and prepare the ingredients and equipment

1. Mix the ingredients to form a dough.
2. Knead until the dough is properly developed. Let the dough rest before rolling and cutting.
3. Roll the pasta dough into thin sheets and cut into the desired shapes. Hold properly if not to be cooked immediately.
4. Evaluate the quality of the finished fresh pasta dough.

Rolling and cutting fresh pasta by machine

Cooking Pasta and Noodles

Key Terms and Concepts

al dente
ravioli press

Basic method

Select and prepare the ingredients and equipment

1. Bring a large amount of water to a rolling boil.
2. Add the pasta and stir it to separate the strands or shapes.
3. Cook the pasta until it is properly cooked and tender. Drain in a colander immediately.
4. (Optional) Rapidly cool and store the pasta. If appropriate or necessary and reheat portions or batches as necessary.
5. Evaluate the quality of the cooked pasta.

General Guidelines

- ➢ pairing pasta with sauces
- ➢ serving fresh and dried pasta
  - à la carte service
  - banquet service
  - buffet service

Chapter 25 Exercises

True/False

Indicate whether each of the following statements is True (T) or False (F)

_____ 1. To hold pasta once it has been cooked, rinse it thoroughly with cold water and toss it in a small amount of oil to keep the strands from clumping together.

_____ 2. In general, fresh pasta cooks faster than dried pasta.

_____ 3. In general, fresh pasta holds better and longer than dried pasta.

_____ 4. Water is the most common cooking liquid for pasta, although stock may be used.

_____ 5. In general, freshly made pasta should be smooth, fairly elastic, and slightly dry to the touch.

_____ 6. Dried pasta can be held in dry storage almost indefinitely.

_____ 7. Fresh pasta can be dried and held in the same way as commercial dried pasta.

_____ 8. Spätzle is a dumpling made from a soft batter that is cut into simmering liquid.

_____ 9. The correct flour to use when making fresh pasta is semolina.

_____ 10. The ratio of water to pasta when cooking fresh pasta is 1 quart water to 1 pound pasta.

Multiple Choice

1. The cooking time for dried pasta in relation to fresh pasta
   a. is longer.
   b. is always shorter.
   c. is about the same.
   d. doesn't matter if the water is at a full boil.

2. The main disadvantage of using fresh pasta is
   a. it has limited shelf life.
   b. it takes longer to cook.
   c. the risk of cross contamination is greater.
   d. it does not offer the variety of shapes or flavors that dried pasta has.

3. One of the advantages of fresh pasta is
   a. it is easier to handle.
   b. it is easier to hold.
   c. it can be shaped and filled as desired.
   d. it takes less time to prepare.

4. When making pasta dough,
   a. salt is added at the end, to make the dough more pliable.
   b. salt is not added because it dries out the dough.
   c. salt is added to the dough to develop flavor.
   d. salt is sprinkled on the dough after it is rolled out.

5. When using vegetables in pasta dough to add flavor and color, they should be
   a. fresh and raw for maximum color.
   b. puréed.
   c. chopped into small pieces.
   d. added at the end of the mixing process.

Fill in the Blank

1. The Italian term _____ is used to describe the proper stage to cook pasta.

2. Excess moisture in pasta dough will cause the dough to be _____. If the dough is too dry, it will be _____.

3. _____ and _____ are examples of long, flat pastas. (Also spaghetti, angel hair, etc.)

4. _____ is coarse-ground flour made from durum wheat often used in pasta dough.

5. The Chinese service of a variety of steamed and fried dumplings is called

   _____.

Matching

_____ 1. semolina   _____ 4. ravioli press

_____ 2. al dente   _____ 5. linguini

_____ 3. tortellini   _____ 6. spätzle

a. pasta cooked until tender but still with a discernible texture

b. machine used to stamp and cut filled pasta

c. ribbon style pasta

d. coarse-ground durum wheat flour used for making pasta

e. filled twisted pasta, usually fresh or frozen

f. soft batter cut into simmering water to make dumplings.

_____ 1. formula   _____ 4. dumpling

_____ 2. ravioli   _____ 5. ziti

_____ 3. fettucini

a. a filled pasta usually cut into circles or squares

b. a broad term generally referring to a batter or dough simmered in liquid.

c. in this context, the base recipe for pasta making

d. a tube pasta made using an extrusion pasta maker

e. ribbon-style pasta

Written/Short Answer

1. What are the differences between dried and fresh pasta?

_____

_____

_____

_____

2. What types of flours can be used to make fresh pasta or noodles?

_____

_____

_____

_____

3. What portion of the egg is used in pasta dough? What are the functions of eggs and oil in a pasta dough?

_____

_____

_____

_____

4. Describe the proper procedure for making, rolling, and cutting fresh pasta.

_____

_____

_____

_____

5. Why are other seasonings added to pasta dough? If added, what precautions should be taken with those ingredients?

_____

_____

_____

_____

6. What is the procedure for holding fresh pasta before cooking?

_____

_____

_____

_____

6. What are dumplings? What are some of the ways that dumpling can be prepared?

_____

_____

_____

_____

Essay

1. Discuss the general guidelines for pairing pasta with sauces. Give some examples.

2. Discuss the general guidelines for serving fresh and dried pasta.

CHAPTER 26

Cooking Eggs

Chapter Overview

According to culinary lore, the chef's hat, with its many pleats, represents the ways that a chef can prepare eggs. They can be served at virtually any meal, as part of every course. They can be cooked in the shell, poached, fried, or scrambled, or prepared as omelets or soufflés; they add flavor and color to other dishes.

Chapter Objectives

After reading and studying this chapter you will be able to

➤ select and prepare eggs (and other ingredients as required) and equipment for specific egg preparations

➤ cook eggs in the shell to a range of doneness and evaluate the quality of eggs cooked in the shell

➤ poach eggs properly and hold them properly for service

➤ fry eggs to a variety of doneness and evaluate their quality according to the appropriate standards

➤ scramble eggs properly and name the characteristics of properly scrambled eggs

➤ identify the different styles of omelet and describe the methods for each style and the their quality characteristics

➤ make a savory soufflé that rises properly and has a light texture

Study Outline

Cooking Eggs in the Shell

Key Terms and Concepts

coddled eggs	green iron sulfide	soft-cooked eggs
deviled eggs	hard-cooked eggs	

Basic Method

Select and prepare the ingredients and equipment

How to cook eggs in the shell

1. Place eggs in a pot with enough water to completely submerge them.
2. Start timing the cooking once the water reaches a simmer and cook to the desired doneness.
3. Evaluate the quality of the cooked eggs.

Poaching Eggs

Key Terms and Concepts

coagulate

eggs Benedict

eggs Florentine

poaching

Basic Method

Select and prepare the ingredients and equipment

1. Bring water, vinegar, and salt to a simmer (180°F/82°C).
2. Add the shelled egg to the simmering water.
3. Remove the egg when done.
4. Evaluate the quality of the poached egg.

Frying Eggs

Key Terms and Concepts

fried eggs American style

frying

huevos rancheros

offset spatula

over easy

over hard

over medium

palette knife

shirred eggs

sunny side up

sur le plat

Basic Method

Select and prepare the ingredients and equipment

1. Heat the pan and the cooking fat over moderate heat.
2. Break the eggs into cups and slide into the hot fat.
3. Cook the eggs until done as desired.
4. Evaluate the quality of the finished fried eggs.

Scrambling Eggs

Key Terms and Concepts

beat	curd	whip
coagulate	scrambling	

Basic Method

Select and prepare the ingredients and equipment

1. Blend the eggs just until the yolks and whites are combined. Add liquid, if using, and seasonings.
2. Preheat the pan and melt the butter. Cook the eggs over low heat.
3. Evaluate the quality of the finished scrambled eggs.

Making Omelets

Key Terms and Concepts

American-style omelet	French-style omelet	rolled omelet
farmer-style omelet	frittata	souffléed omelet
flat omelet	puffy omelet	tortilla

Basic Method

Select and prepare the ingredients and equipment

1. Blend the eggs with any liquid, if using, salt, pepper, and seasonings.
   - For rolled, folded, or flat omelets
   - For souffléd omelets
2. Heat the pan and then add the oil or butter over high heat or in a hot oven. Add any appropriate garnishes at this time.
3. Add the eggs and cook the omelet until the eggs are properly set. Add any additional fillings or garnishes, if desired.
   - For individually prepared rolled and folded omelets
   - Individual flat omelets
   - Souffléed omelets
4. Evaluate the quality of the finished omelet.

How to Roll a French-Style Omelet

➢ Spread or flatten the omelet to an even layer

➢ Roll the edge nearest the handle toward the center

➢ Shake the pan

➢ Roll the omelet out of the pan onto a heated plate

Savory Soufflés

Key Terms and Concepts

béchamel	soufflé	tempering
soft peaks	soufflé base	

Basic Method

Select and prepare the ingredients and equipment

1. Prepare the base and incorporate any additional ingredients and seasonings.
2. Whip the egg whites to soft peaks. Fold the egg whites into the base
3. Fill the prepared molds as soon as the egg whites are folded into the base.
4. Place the soufflés immediately in a hot (425°F/220°C) oven and bake until risen, cooked through, and browned.
5. Serve the soufflé immediately.
6. Evaluate the quality of the finished soufflé.

Chapter 26 Exercises

True/False

Indicate whether each of the following statements is True (T) or False(F)

_____ 1. Approximately 2 ounces base and 2 ounces egg whites are used for 1 individual soufflé.

_____ 2. *Sur le plat* is French for rolled omelet.

_____ 3. Moisture weeping from scrambled eggs indicates the eggs were overcooked.

_____ 4. Adding a small amount of water to eggs before scrambling will make them puffier.

_____ 5. The ideal temperature for frying an egg is the same range at which butter sizzles without turning brown.

_____ 6. Hard-cooked eggs are easier to peel once they have cooled down.

_____ 7. The best way to prevent the green ring from forming in hard-cooked eggs is to not allow the eggs to boil longer than necessary.

_____ 8. When poaching, eggs should be added when the water is 165°F/73°C.

_____ 9. Soufflés should be baked in an oven heated to 425°F/220°C.

_____ 10. The ideal temperature range for frying eggs is 180 to 212°F/82 to 100°C.

Multiple Choice

1. When cooking eggs, very fresh eggs are recommended for all the following preparations, except:
   a. poached
   b. hard boiled
   c. fried
   d. scrambled

2. Coddled eggs are an example of which technique?
   a. Poached
   b. Cooked in the shell
   c. Fried
   d. Scrambled

3. Shirred eggs most resemble which technique?
   a. Poached
   b. Cooked in the shell
   c. Fried
   d. Scrambled

4. A tortilla is an example of which technique?
   a. Huevos rancheros
   b. Shirred
   c. Rolled omelet
   d. Flat omelet

5. Eggs Florentine is an egg dish prepared by which technique?

a. Poached
b. Cooked in the shell
c. Fried
d. Scrambled

Fill in the Blank

1. Two tools used to make turning fried eggs easier are _____ and _____.

2. Eggs Benedict is an example the _____technique. Huevos rancheros are an example of the _____technique.

3. When whipping egg whites for soufflés, they should be beaten to the _____ stage.

4. Puffy or _____omelets are prepared with beaten egg whites.

5. The basic components of any soufflé, sweet or savory, are _____and _____.

Matching

_____ 1. over easy   _____ 4. soft peaks

_____ 2. scrambled   _____ 5. tortilla

_____ 3. soft cooked   _____ 6. rolled omelet

a. a Spanish-style flat omelet

b. beaten eggs stirred in a pan over low heat to form a curd

c. a French-style omelet

d. egg cooked in the shell in simmering water for 3 to 4 minutes

e. an early stage of beaten egg whites, used for soufflé preparations

f. a fried egg which is turned

_____ 1. frittata   _____ 4. coddled

_____ 2. shirred   _____ 5. soufflé

_____ 3. eggs Benedict

a. dish featuring poached eggs

b. a savory dish prepared with beaten egg whites, or a type of omele

c. an Italian-style flat omelet

d. egg cooked in the shell in simmering water for about 30 seconds

e. a shelled egg cooked in the oven with garnishes, in the French style

Written/Short Answer

1. What are the different types of omelets and how are each prepared?

    _____

    _____

    _____

    _____

2. How are eggs cooked in the shell?

    _____

    _____

    _____

    _____

3. What is the cooking medium for poaching eggs? Why?

    _____

    _____

    _____

    _____

4. How can poached eggs be prepared for restaurant service?

    _____

    _____

    _____

    _____

5. What are the two ways to make scrambled eggs? When are garnishes added?

    _____

    _____

    _____

    _____

6. How is a French-style omelet rolled?

_____

_____

_____

_____

7. Briefly describe how to fry an egg American-style, sunny-side-up and over.

_____

_____

_____

_____

Essay

1. How does timing affect soufflé preparation? What does the kitchen rule "the customer waits for the soufflé, the soufflé does not wait for the customer" imply?

2. According to the text, "the simplicity of the poached egg is its greatest asset, but as every chef knows, the simpler the dish, the more the chef's skill is on display." What does this mean and how does it apply to you as a culinary student?

CHAPTER **27**

SALAD DRESSINGS AND SALADS

Chapter Overview

A vinaigrette is a cold sauce typically made from three parts oil and one part vinegar. Good quality oils and vinegars can be infused with spices, aromatics, herbs, and fruits or vegetables and used in a variety of applications, including salad dressings, or on their own as a condiment. Mayonnaise is cold sauce made by combining egg yolks with oil to form a stable emulsion. Unlike vinaigrette, this sauce does not break as it sits.

In its most basic form, a green salad (sometimes called a tossed salad, mixed salad, or garden salad) is made of one or more salad greens tossed with a dressing. A wide variety of other salads (fruit, warm, grain, potato, pasta, grain, legume, and composed) are also made in the professional kitchen.

Chapter Objectives

After reading and studying this chapter, you will be able to

➢ use the basic ratios and methods to prepare vinaigrettes and mayonnaise

➢ describe how to rescue a broken mayonnaise

➢ evaluate the quality of salad dressings according to the correct quality standards

➢ name the purposes for a green salad

➢ select and combine salad greens and wash, dry, and store them properly

➢ make croutons properly

➢ prepare flavored oils and vinegars and store them properly

➢ select and prepare a variety of fresh fruits for salads

➢ select and prepare ingredients and dressings for warm, vegetable, potato, pasta, grain, legume, and composed salads

Study Outline

Vinaigrette

Key Terms and Concepts

cold sauce
dressing
emulsion/emulsifier

homogenous
marinade
temporary emulsion

vinaigrette

Basic Method

Select and prepare the ingredients and equipment

1. Combine the vinegar with the emulsifying and seasoning ingredients.
2. Add the oil.
3. Add any garnish and adjust the seasoning.
4. Evaluate the quality of the finished vinaigrette.

Flavored Oils and Vinegars

To infuse oils and vinegars use one of the following methods

➢ Heat

➢ Strain

➢ Purée

➢ Combine

➢ Rest

Mayonnaise

Key Terms and Concepts

aïoli
base sauce
foodborne illness
grand sauce

lecithin
mayonnaise
pasteurized egg yolks
rémoulade

sauce vert
tartar sauce

Basic Method

Select and prepare the ingredients and equipment

Make the mayonnaise
1. Blend the yolks with a bit of water.
2. Add the oil a little at a time, whisking it in completely.
3. Adjust the thickness and flavor of the sauce by adding a bit more acid or water when incorporating the oil.
4. Add any additional flavoring or garnish ingredients at the point indicated in the recipe.
5. Evaluate the quality of the finished mayonnaise.

Green Salads

Key Terms and Concepts

bruschetta	croustades	rusks
chicory	heading greens	spinner
crostini	hydroponically-raised greens	
croutons	mesclun greens	

Basic Method

Select and prepare the ingredients and equipment

➢ mild and spicy greens

➢ bitter greens and chicories

➢ prepared mixes and blends of greens

➢ herbs and flowers

Make the green salad

1. Wash the greens thoroughly in plenty of cool water to remove all traces of dirt or sand.
2. Dry the greens completely.
3. Store cleaned greens in tubs or other containers.
4. Cut or tear the lettuce into bite-size pieces.
5. Garnish and dress the salad.

Fruit Salads

Key Terms and Concepts

acidulated water

blanch

box grater

citrus suprêmes

cross contamination

extractor

functional garnish

juice/juicing

mandoline

membranes

oxidize

pith

reamer

zest/zester

Apples

Citrus Fruits

Mango

Pineapple

Melons

Warm Salads

Vegetable Salads

Potato Salads

Pasta and Grain Salads

Legume Salads

Composed Salads

- Consider how well each of the elements combine. Contrasting flavors are intriguing. Conflicting flavors are a disaster.
- Repetition of a color or flavor can be successful if it contributes to the overall dish. But generally, too much of a good thing is simply too much.
- Each element of the dish should be so perfectly prepared that it could easily stand on its own. However, each part is enhanced by being in combination with the others.
- Components should be arranged in such a way that the textures and colors of the foods are most attractive to the eye.

Chapter 27 Exercises

True/False

Indicate whether each of the following statements is True (T) or False(F)

_____ 1. The main purpose of holding apples in acidulated water is to keep them from drying out.

_____ 2. Classic recipes for mayonnaise call for 6 to 8 ounces of oil to each egg yolk.

_____ 3. *Salade tiède* is the French term for green salads.

_____ 4. When making vinaigrette, very strongly flavored oils are usually blended with less intense oils.

_____ 5. When blending mayonnaise, additional lemon juice, vinegar, or water are added as the mayonnaise becomes thick in order to allow it to absorb more oil.

_____ 6. Vinaigrette is a cold sauce typically made from 2 parts oil to 1 part vinegar.

_____ 7. Vinaigrettes whipped together by hand hold their emulsion longer than those that are made by machine do.

_____ 8. Properly prepared vinaigrette will separate as it sits.

_____ 9. Mustard is the most commonly used emulsifier when preparing mayonnaise.

_____ 10. When preparing flavored oils and vinegars, you must heat the oil or vinegar first.

Multiple Choice

1. Vinaigrette is a cold sauce typically made from
   a. 2 parts oil to 1 part vinegar.
   b. 3 parts oil to 1 part vinegar.
   c. an oil and egg yolk emulsion.
   d. dressings and marinades.

2. When making vinaigrette, very strongly flavored oils
   a. should not be used.
   b. should be blended with less intense oils.
   c. should only be used for marinades.
   d. will inhibit the emulsification process.

3. When making vinaigrette, the correct procedure is
   a. combining the oil with the emulsifier and seasonings, then adding the oil.
   b. combining the vinegar with the emulsifier and seasonings, then adding the oil.
   c. combining the vinegar with the oil, the adding the emulsifying ingredient to blend.
   d. combining vinegar, oil, and emulsifier, and then adding the seasoning ingredients.

4. A properly prepared vinaigrette
   a. will remain homogenous under refrigeration for long periods of time.
   b. should be used immediately.
   c. will quickly begin to separate.
   d. will remain homogenous if heated to a simmer and then held under refrigeration.

5. Classic recipes for mayonnaise call for
   a. 2 ounces of oil to each egg yolk.
   b. 4 to 6 ounces of oil to each egg yolk.
   c. 6 to 8 ounces of oil to each egg yolk.
   d. 8 to 10 ounces of oil to each egg yolk.

Fill in the Blank

1. A decorative cut where a half mango is scored in a crosshatch pattern and then turned inside out is known as the _____.

2. When peeling an apple, a _____ should be used. It is easiest to peel a pineapple using a _____.

3. _____ is the outer brightly colored portion of the citrus fruit's peel or rind. The underlying white _____ has a bitter taste.

4. To remove any unpleasant bitter taste of zest, it can be _____.

5. Classic recipes for mayonnaise call for _____ ounces of oil to each egg yolk.

Matching

_____ 1. zest   _____ 4. emulsifier

_____ 2. membrane   _____ 5. reamer

_____ 3. aïoli   _____ 6. chicory

a. the connective tissue which encases each citrus segment
b. a type of bitter green
c. the outer portion of a citrus fruit's peel or rind
d. an ingredient which is used to bind together two ingredients into a homogenous blend
e. garlic mayonnaise
f. a tool used to juice citrus fruits

_____ 1. suprêmes   _____ 4. vinaigrette

_____ 2. pith   _____ 5. mayonnaise

_____ 3. extractor

a. the white, bitter portion of the skin of citrus fruit
b. a tool used to juice citrus fruits
c. egg yolks and oil combined to form an emulsion
d. citrus segments which are free of membrane
e. a cold sauce composed of 3 parts oil to 1 part vinegar

Written/Short Answer

1. Explain how to save a broken mayonnaise.

_____

_____

_____

_____

2. For vegetable salads, what are the two methods for combining partially or fully cooked vegetables with dressing? Why might you select each particular method?

_____

_____

_____

_____

3. What are the basic ingredients in vinaigrettes? Briefly explain how to make a vinaigrette.

_____

_____

_____

_____

4. What are the basic ingredients in mayonnaise? Briefly explain how to make a mayonnaise.

_____

_____

_____

5. What are the different methods to make flavored oils and vinegars?

_____

_____

_____

_____

6. What are the general categories of greens? How are they paired with dressings?

_____

_____

_____

_____

7. How are croutons made?

_____

_____

_____

_____

Essay

1. What are composed salads and what are the general principals to follow when preparing them? Give 2 examples of well-known composed salads.

2. What are flavored oils and vinegars? Why would a chef make them, and how are they used?

CHAPTER 28

Chapter Overview

Sandwiches find their place on nearly every menu, from elegant receptions and teas to substantial but casual meals. Built from four simple elements–bread, a spread, a filling, and a garnish–they exemplify the ways in which a global approach to cuisine can result in nearly endless variety.

A sandwich can be open or closed, hot or cold. Cold sandwiches include standard deli-style versions made from sliced meats or mayonnaise-dressed salads. Finger and tea sandwiches are delicate items made on fine-grained bread, trimmed of their crusts and precisely cut into shapes and sizes that can be eaten in about two average bites. Club sandwiches, also known as triple decker sandwiches, are included in this category as well. Hot sandwiches may feature a hot filling, such as hamburgers or pastrami. Others are grilled, like a Reuben sandwich or a melt. Sometimes a hot filling is mounded on bread and the sandwich is topped with a hot sauce.

Chapter Objectives

After reading and studying this chapter, you will be able to

➤ name the basic components of a sandwich and describe the function of each component in the finished sandwich

➤ prepare a flavored butter

➤ describe some of the ways that sandwiches can be presented

➤ select sandwich shapes to maximize yield and lower food cost

➤ organize your work station to prepare and serve sandwiches for maximum productivity and efficiency

Study Outline

Elements in a Sandwich

Key Terms and Concepts

canapé	entrée	garnish
closed sandwich	fat-based spread	hors-d'oeuvre
club sandwich	filling	open-faced sandwich
crumb	finger sandwich	spread
deli-style sandwich	flavored butter	straight-edge sandwiches

tea sandwich   triple decker sandwich

Breads

Pullman loaves   Flatbreads
Peasant-style breads   Wrappers
Rolls   Flour and corn tortillas

Spreads

Mayonnaise or creamy salad dressing   Tahini and nut butters
Plain or compound butters   Jelly, jam, compotes, chutneys, and other fruit
Mustard or ketchup   preserves
Spreadable cheeses   Avocado pulp or guacamole
Vegetable or herb spreads   Oils and vinaigrettes

Fillings

Sliced roasted or simmered meats   Grilled, pan-fried, or broiled burgers, sausages,
Sliced cheeses   fish, or poultry
Grilled, roasted, or fresh vegetables Salads of meats, poultry, eggs, fish, or
                                           vegetables

Garnishes

Green salad or side salad   Pickle spears or olives
Lettuce and sprouts   Dips, spreads, or relishes
Sliced fresh vegetables   Sliced fruits

Presentation Styles

Sandwich Production Guidelines

➢ Organize the work so that it moves in a direct line.

➢ Prepare spreads prior to service and have them at a spreadable consistency. Use a spatula to spread the entire surface of the bread.

➢ Slice breads and rolls prior to service for volume production. Whenever possible, toast, grill, or broil breads when ready to assemble the sandwich. If bread must be toasted in advance, hold the toast in a warm area, loosely covered.

➢ Prepare and portion fillings and garnishes in advance and hold them at the correct temperature. Clean and dry lettuce or other greens in advance.

➢ Grilled sandwiches such as a Reuben sandwich or Croques Monsieur can be fully assembled in advance of service, then grilled or heated to order.

Chapter 28 Exercises

True/False

Indicate whether each of the following statements is True (T) or False(F)

_____ 1.   The tight crumb of peasant-style bread makes it a good choice for tea and finger sandwiches.

_____ 2.   The yield is generally lower when preparing straight-edge sandwiches, making them slightly more expensive to produce.

_____ 3.   The garnish becomes part of the sandwich's overall structure, so it should complement or contrast the main filling.

_____ 4.   The filling should determine how all the other elements of the sandwich are selected and prepared.

_____ 5.   Spreads should be simple and subtly flavored.

_____ 6.   Most breads can be sliced in advance of sandwich preparation as long as they are carefully covered to prevent drying out.

_____ 7.   Flavored butters are prepared by hand, compound butters are prepared with a mixer or food processor.

_____ 8.   Because of their delicate nature, tea sandwiches should be cut as close to service time as possible.

_____ 9.   Breads can be successfully toasted two hours in advance of service without any loss in quality.

_____ 10. The spread can be applied directly to the bread or combined with the filling before preparing the sandwich.

Multiple Choice

1. For tea sandwiches, it is important to consider the crumb of the bread because of its
    a. flavor.
    b. appearance.
    c. slicing capability.

    d. holding capability.

2. The recommended bread for tea or finger sandwiches is
    a. Pullman loaves.
    b. peasant-style loaves.
    c. flatbreads.
    d. tortillas.

3. Lavash is an example of
    a. spreadable cheese.
    b. nut butter.
    c. relish.
    d. flatbread.

4. Most breads can be sliced in advance of sandwich preparation as long as they are
    a. carefully covered to prevent drying.
    b. Pullman loaves.
    c. toasted in advance.
    d. refrigerated.

5. In sandwich making, ciabatta is a type of
    a. bread.
    b. spread.
    c. filling.
    d. garnish.

Fill in the Blank

1. To maximize the work flow to eliminate unnecessary movement, organize the work in a
_____.

2. To maximize the work flow to eliminate unnecessary movement, the best tool to apply a spread would be a _____.

3. A finger sandwich served as an hors d'oeuvre is a type of _____.

4. A club sandwich is a type of _____ sandwich.

5. When a hot filling is mounded on bread and the sandwich is topped with a hot sauce, this is an example of a _____.

Matching

_____ 1. canapé   _____ 4. crumb
_____ 2. triple decker sandwich   _____ 5. fat-based spread
_____ 3. open-faced sandwich   _____ 6. garnish

a. grain and texture of the bread
b. club sandwich
c. mayonnaise or butter
d. sandwich addition that complements or contrasts with the filling
e. sandwich with only one side of bread serving as a base
f. bite-size hors d'oeuvre

_____ 1. tea sandwich   _____ 4. filling
_____ 2. flavored butter   _____ 5. closed sandwich
_____ 3. spread

a. the focus of the sandwich
b. finger sandwich
c. compound butter
d. acts as a barrier to keep the bread from getting soggy
e. a sandwich with two slices of bread

Written/Short Answer

1. What are the elements of a sandwich and what are the different types and service of sandwiches?

_____

_____

_____

_____

2. List 5 types of breads and give 2 examples of sandwiches typically prepared with each.

_____

_____

_____

_____

_____

3. List 5 types of spreads and give 2 examples of sandwiches typically prepared with each.

_____

_____

_____

_____

4. List 5 types of fillings and give 2 examples of sandwiches typically prepared with each.

_____

_____

_____

_____

5. List 5 types of fillings and give 2 examples of sandwiches typically prepared with each.

_____

_____

_____

_____

6. How are flavored butters made and what are the primary uses for the butter?

_____

_____

_____

_____

7. Explain garnishes and what are two main ways they are presented?

_____

_____

_____

_____

Essay

1. Name some ways to eliminate any unnecessary movement in sandwich production.

2. Briefly explain production of canapés, finger, and tea sandwiches.

CHAPTER 29

Hors-d'Oeuvre and Appetizers

Chapter Overview

The distinction between an hors-d'oeuvre and an appetizer has more to do with how and when it is served than with the actual food being served. Hors-d'oeuvre are typically served as a prelude to a meal. They are meant to pique the taste buds and perk up the appetite. While hors-d'oeuvre are served separately from the main meal, appetizers are traditionally its first course.

Chapter Objectives

After reading and studying this chapter, you will be able to

➤ list the basic differences and similarities between appetizers and hors-d'oeuvre

➤ select and prepare ingredients, preparations, and garnishes for hors-d'oeuvre, appetizers, and cold savory mousses

➤ describe the qualities of foods to be served as appetizers

➤ present hors-d'oeuvre properly

➤ name the basic guidelines for preparing and preserving appetizers

➤ work properly with gelatin in order to achieve specific effects

Study Outline

Hors-d'oeuvre

Key Terms and Concepts

buffet	chafing dish	ice carving
butler-style service	hors-d'oeuvre	"outside the meal"
canapé	ice bed	teasing the appetite

Foods served as hors-d'oeuvre should be

- Perfectly fresh.
- Small enough to eat in one or two bites.
- Attractive.
- Designed to complement the meal that is to follow.

Presenting hors-d'oeuvre

- Keep in mind the nature of the event as well as the menu that follows when selecting hors-d'oeuvre.
- Ice carvings and ice beds are often used to keep seafood and caviar very cold as well as for their dramatic appeal.
- Hors-d'oeuvre served on platters or passed on trays should be thoughtfully presented, so that the last hors-d'oeuvre on the plate is still attractively presented.
- Hors-d'oeuvre that are served with a sauce require serving utensils.
- To ensure that hot hors-d'oeuvre stay hot, avoid combining hot and cold items on a single platter and have chafing dishes available for buffet service.

Appetizers

Key Terms and Concepts

appetizer	galantine	sampler plate
building a menu	garnish	terrine
crêpes	pâté	vols au vent

Preparing and Presenting Appetizers

- Keep the portion size appropriate.
- Season all appetizers with meticulous care.
- Keep garnishes to a minimum.
- Serve all appetizers at the proper temperature.
- Slice, shape, and portion appetizers carefully with just enough to make the appetizer interesting and appealing from start to finish but not so much on the plate that the guest is overwhelmed.
- Neatness always counts, but especially with appetizers.
- When offering shared appetizers, consider how they will look when they come to the table.
- Color, shape, and white space play a role in the overall composition of the plate.

Cold Savory Mousse

Key Terms and Concepts

aerator	cold mousse	mousse
aspic	gel strength	spread
binder	gelatin	tartlet mold
bloom	lightener	

Basic Method

Select and prepare the ingredients and equipment

Make the mousse

➢ Prepare the main ingredients.

➢ Add the gelatin, if necessary.

➢ Fold in the whipped cream and/or egg whites.

➢ The mousse is ready to mold now.

➢ Evaluate the quality of the finished mousse.

Working with powdered gelatin

➢ Weigh the gelatin carefully.

➢ Rain or sprinkle gelatin powder over a cool liquid. If the liquid is warm or hot, the gelatin will not soften properly. Scattering the gelatin over the surface of the liquid prevents the gelatin from forming clumps.

➢ As the gelatin absorbs the liquid, each granule becomes enlarged. This is known as blooming.

➢ Warm the gelatin over a hot water bath or in a microwave on low power to dissolve the granules. As the softened gelatin warms, the mixture will clear and become liquid enough to pour easily.

Chapter 29 Exercises

True/False

Indicate whether each of the following statements is True (T) or False(F)

_____ 1. Hors-d'oeuvre can be prepared from small pieces and trim from food used elsewhere in the kitchen.

_____ 2. Cheese-based mousses are often stable enough that they don't require a binder such as gelatin.

_____ 3. A food processor should not be used when preparing a main item for the base of the mousse as it will turn the main item into a thick paste.

_____ 4. All appetizers should be served at the correct temperature, on chilled plates.

_____ 5. Fresh clams and oysters make excellent appetizer choices because they can be shucked and portioned in advance.

_____ 6. Before dissolving the gelatin granules in warm water, they should be stirred into the base.

_____ 7. The French word mousse literally translates into "foam or froth."

_____ 8. In general, appetizers are smaller than hors-d'oeuvre.

_____ 9. When preparing mousse, the purpose of adding velouté or béchamel would be to thicken the base.

_____ 10. Hors-d'oeuvre can be served butler-style, buffet, or a combination of service styles.

Multiple Choice

1. The French term hors-d'oeuvre literally translates as
   a. teasing the appetite.
   b. first course.
   c. outside the meal.
   d. appetizer.

2. Because hors-d'oeuvre customarily precede a meal, they
   a. should have a similar taste or texture as the meal.
   b. should not include a sauce.
   c. should always be served hot.
   d. should tease the appetite.

3. Appetizers are traditionally served as the
   a. hors-d'oeuvre.
   b. sampler plate.
   c. first course.
   d. second course.

4. Classic hors-d'oeuvre can be served as appetizers by
   a. serving them hot.
   b. plating them individually rather than passing them.
   c. serving them with utensils.

    d. increasing their size.

5. The French word mousse literally translates into
    a. foam, froth.
    b. light, airy.
    c. hollow.
    d. whipped.

Fill in the Blank

1. Before adding the gelatin to the base, the base must be cooled, if necessary, to _____
   _____.

2. Gelatin granules will dissolve in liquid warmed to _____.

3. The correct gel strength for preparing cold mousse is _____.

4. The correct ratio of gel to liquid for preparing cold mousse is _____
   gel to _____liquid.

5. If a purée of vegetables is used in mousse preparation, it may need to be sautéed to
   _____and _____.

Matching

_____ 1. mousse   _____ 4. hors-d'oeuvre
_____ 2. gel strength   _____ 5. aerator
_____ 3. firm gel   _____ 6. gelatin

a. gel strength for cold mousse
b. French for "outside the meal"
c. foam of whipped egg whites or whipped cream
d. French for "foam or froth"
e. used to bind, stabilize foams, and thicken liquids that will be served cold
f. concentration of gelatin

_____ 1. blooming   _____ 4. lightener
_____ 2. drum sieve   _____ 5. hors-d'oeuvre
_____ 3. binder

a. usually necessary ingredient in mousse; gelatin is one
b. tool used to strain
c. small course to tease the appetite

d. the process of softening the gel

e. foam of whipped egg whites or whipped cream

Written/Short Answer

1. What are the basic ingredients for mousse and give some examples?

_____

_____

_____

_____

2. Briefly describe how to make a mousse.

_____

_____

_____

_____

3. What are some guidelines to choosing ingredients for and preparing hors-d'oeuvre?

_____

_____

_____

_____

4. Name 5 examples of appetizers and 5 examples of hors-d'oeuvre.

_____

_____

_____

_____

5. What are the uses for gelatin?

_____

_____

_____

6. What are the formulas for the four main gel strengths?

_____

_____

_____

_____

7. Briefly describe how do you prepare gelatin?

_____

_____

_____

_____

Essay

1. What are some guidelines for presenting hors-d'oeuvre?

2. What are some guidelines for preparing and presenting appetizers?

CHAPTER **30**

Chapter Overview

Charcuterie, strictly speaking, refers to certain foods made from the pig, including sausage, smoked ham, bacon, head cheese, pâtés, and terrines. Garde manger traditionally referred to the kitchen's pantry or larder section, where foods were kept cold during extended storage, as well as while being prepared as a cold presentation.

Forcemeat, a basic component of such charcuterie and garde manger preparations as pâtés and terrines, is prepared by grinding lean meats together with fat and seasonings to form an emulsion.

Chapter Objectives

After reading and studying this chapter, you will be able to

➢ define charcuterie and garde manger

➢ explain what a forcemeat is

➢ select and prepare ingredients, preparations, and equipment necessary to prepare a variety of forcemeats and forcemeat-based dishes

➢ sample a forcemeat by preparing a quenelle

➢ name and describe four forcemeats

➢ fill and line a mold for terrines and pâtés

➢ evaluate the quality of finished items prepared from forcemeats

Study Outline

Forcemeats

Key Terms and Concepts

aspic gelée
béchamel
binder
charcuterie
country-style forcemeat
die
drum sieve
emulsion
feed tube
forcemeat

galantine
garde manger
gratin forcemeat
liaison
liner
meat grinder
mousseline-style forcemeat
panada
pâté
pâte à choux

pâté en croûte
pâté mold
quenelle
straight forcemeat
stuffing
tamis
tamper
terrine
worm

Basic Method

Select and prepare the ingredients and equipment

1. Follow sound sanitation procedures and maintain cold temperatures at all times.
2. Grind foods properly.
3. Once properly ground, mix or process the ingredients, combining the ground meat with a secondary binder, if desired.
4. Push the forcemeat through a drum sieve, if necessary.
5. Taste test the forcemeat for flavor and consistency.
6. The forcemeat is ready to garnish, if desired, and use as a stuffing or filling, or it may be placed into a prepared mold and cooked.
7. Evaluate the quality of the finished forcemeat.

Chapter 30 Exercises

True/False

Indicate whether each of the following statements is True (T) or False(F)

_____ 1.   To prepare a bread panada, use 2 parts bread to 1 part milk.

_____ 2.   A mousseline-style forcemeat is prepared by combining ground meats with prepared mousse.

_____ 3. Fatback and heavy cream are types of fat that might be included in a forcemeat preparation.

_____ 4. Salt should be added to forcemeats in small amounts, as the natural salt of the meat will generally provide enough seasoning.

_____ 5. It is important to test quenelles at the temperature at which they will be served.

_____ 6. Garnishes may be either folded into the forcemeat or arranged in the terrine.

_____ 7. Pâte à choux is sometimes used as a binder for forcemeat.

_____ 8. A liaison of cream and eggs may be used to bind the forcemeat.

_____ 9. A panada is an ingredient that provides richness, smoothness, and moisture to the cooked forcemeat.

_____ 10. Gelatin sheets are sometimes used to line the terrine mold for forcemeats to give added moisture and freshness.

Multiple Choice

1. A straight forcemeat typically is composed of
   a. lean meats ground with fatback.
   b. coarse-textured forcemeat containing liver.
   c. seared meat ground with other ingredients.
   d. delicate meats combined with cream and eggs.

2. A mousseline-style forcemeat typically is composed of
   a. lean meats ground with fatback.
   b. coarse-textured forcemeat containing liver.
   c. seared meat ground with other ingredients.
   d. delicate meats combined with cream and eggs.

3. A country-style forcemeat typically is composed of
   a. lean meats ground with fatback.
   b. coarse-textured forcemeat containing liver.
   c. seared meat ground with other ingredients.
   d. delicate meats combined with cream and eggs.

4. A gratin forcemeat typically is composed of
   a. lean meats ground with fatback.
   b. coarse-textured forcemeat containing liver.
   c. seared meat ground with other ingredients.
   d. delicate meats combined with cream and eggs.

5. The three basic components of forcemeat are
   a. meat, fat, seasonings.
   b. meat, vegetables, fat.
   c. meat, fatback, salt.
   d. meat, cream, seasonings.

Fill in the Blank

1. _____ is a well-seasoned, highly gelatinous, clarified stock applied to forcemeats to preserve their moisture and freshness.

2. Panadas, eggs, and heavy cream, are all examples of forcemeat _____, which hold the forcemeat together.

3. _____, strictly speaking, refers to certain foods made from the pig: sausage, smoked ham, bacon, pâtés, and terrines.

4. _____ typically has a coarser texture than most forcemeats and contains liver.

5. A drum sieve, also known as _____, is used to produce a fine and delicate textured forcemeat.

Matching

_____ 1. quenelle   _____ 4. panada
_____ 2. mousseline forcemeat   _____ 5. pâté en croûte
_____ 3. tamis   _____ 6. straight forcemeat

a. a forcemeat baked in a pastry-lined mold
b. drum sieve
c. delicate forcemeat made with cream and eggs
d. forcemeat dumpling
e. lean meat ground together with fat
f. binder usually made with bread or flour

_____ 1. binder   _____ 4. aspic gelée
_____ 2. liner   _____ 5. gratin forcemeat
_____ 3. country-style forcemeat

a. highly gelatinous, clarified stock
b. forcemeat containing seared ground meat
c. coarse-textured forcemeat usually containing liver

d. panada, eggs, or pâte à choux

e. pastry, fatback, and prosciutto

Written/Short Answer

1. Name the four types of forcemeat and how they differ.

_____

_____

_____

_____

2. What are the three basic components of forcemeat? Explain the purpose of each.

_____

_____

_____

_____

3. Briefly describe the basic preparation of forcemeat.

_____

_____

_____

_____

4. What is a binder and when is it used? Give some examples.

_____

_____

_____

_____

5. What are they types of panadas? Why are they used?

_____

_____

_____

_____

6. Name some types of garnishes. When are they added to the forcemeat?

_____

_____

_____

_____

7. Name some types of liners. When and how are they used?

_____

_____

_____

_____

Essay

1. What are the two reasons ingredients and equipment for forcemeat preparation must be kept well chilled? Discuss how this is accomplished.

2. What is the purpose of testing the forcemeat and how is it done?

CHAPTER **31**

Chapter Overview

The ingredients used in many baked items fulfill several different functions, giving the finished baked item stability, tenderness, sweetness, leavening, thickening, and adding flavor. Baking depends on exact measurements and precise handling of ingredients and tools to assure quality and consistency. Scaling and sifting dry ingredients, pan and oven preparation, and the use of a pastry tip are fundamental skills in the bakeshop. Sugar is cooked to various stages to make simple syrup or caramel; cream may be whipped to a range of peaks; egg whites are made into a variety of meringues.

Chapter Objectives

After reading and studying this chapter, you will be able to

➢ describe the different functions of ingredients in baked items: stability, tenderness, sweetness, leavening, thickening, and flavoring

➢ explain the importance of accurate measurements in baking

➢ scale dry and wet ingredients properly, using the appropriate measuring equipment

➢ sift dry ingredients properly

➢ select and prepare pans and ovens for a variety of baked goods

➢ prepare and use of a pastry bag and tips

➢ cook sugar to various stages to make simple syrup or caramel

➢ whip cream and egg whites to a range of peaks

➢ name the basic types of meringues and prepare meringues according to the proper method

Study Outline

The Functions of Ingredients in Baking

Key Terms and Concepts

acid
active dry yeast
alkali
baking fats
chemical leavener
combination mixing method
compressed yeast
crumb
flavoring
foaming method

fresh yeast
gelatin
gluten
instant yeast
leaveners
organic leavener
physical leavener
quick breads
shorteners
stabilizer

starch granules
starches
strengthener
sourdough starter
sucrose
sweetener
tenderizer
thickener

Thickeners

- Arrowroot and cornstarch
- Flour
- Eggs
- Gelatin

Scaling

Key Terms and Concepts

balance-beam scale
electronic scale

scale out
scaling

spring-type scale

Sifting

Key Terms and Concepts

aerates
parchment paper

sieve
sift

Cooking Sugar

Key Terms and Concepts

candy thermometer
caramel

crystallization
firm ball stage

hard ball stage
hard crack stage

invert sugar   simple syrup   soft crack
poaching medium   soft ball stage   thread

Simple syrup

Cooking sugar to various stages

A few basic rules apply when cooking sugar.
- Use a heavy gauge pot.
- Add an acid or an invert sugar.
- Brush down the pot with a moist pastry brush.
- Warm milk or other liquids before adding to caramel.
- Add all liquids carefully, away from heat.

Whipped Cream or Chantilly Cream

Key Terms and Concepts

chantilly cream   medium peak   whipped cream
firm peak   soft peak

Whipping Egg Whites and Making Meringues

Key Terms and Concepts

common meringue   leavener   meringue
Italian meringue   lightener   Swiss meringue

Separating Whole Eggs

Choosing and Preparing Pans

Key Terms and Concepts

dusting pans
greasing pan
ungreased pans

Selecting and Preparing Ovens

Key Terms and Concepts

convection oven
conventional oven
steam-injected oven

Cooling and Storing Baked Goods

Key Terms and Concepts

cooling on racks
reheating
refreshing

Using pastry Bags and Tips

Key Terms and Concepts

coupler   piping   tip
pastry bag   portioning tool

Chapter 31 Exercises

True/False

Indicate whether each of the following statements is True (T) or False(F)

_____ 1. Active dry yeast can be substituted for compressed yeast in equal amounts.

_____ 2. Eggs act as stabilizers, shorteners, and/or thickeners in baked goods.

_____ 3. Flour acts as a stabilizer, shortener, and/or thickener in the bakeshop.

_____ 4. Items are scaled in the bakeshop primarily when preparing large volumes of pastries or breads.

_____ 5. The tool most often used in a professional bakeshop to sift ingredients is a sieve.

_____ 6. Unlike organic leaveners, chemical leaveners take a substantial amount of time to do their work.

_____ 7. Fresh and compressed yeast must be held under refrigerator; dry and instant yeast can be held without refrigeration in dry storage.

_____ 8. Heavy cream whipped to a stiff peak is typically used in sauce to pool under or be spooned over a dessert.

_____ 9. Cream whipped to a medium peak is typically used to cover cakes or garnish items.

_____ 10. Egg whites can be beaten in advance and held for up to 30 minutes under refrigeration without losing their volume.

Multiple Choice

1. The protein in flour that is important in yeast bread production is
    a. fermentation.
    b. wheat.
    c. gluten.
    d. starch.

2. Egg whites whip to the greatest volume when they are
    a. chilled.
    b. at room temperature.
    c. heated to 105°F/40°C.
    d. heated to 140°F/60°C.

3. Eggs separate most easily when they are
    a. chilled.
    b. at room temperature.
    c. heated to 105°F/40°C.
    d. heated to 140°F/60°C.

4. A meringue that is prepared by beating the egg whites until frothy and then gradually adding the sugar is called a
    a. common meringue.
    b. Italian meringue.
    c. French meringue.
    d. Swiss meringue.

5. A meringue that is prepared by combining the egg whites and sugar in a mixing bowl over a bain marie and then whipping to the desired stage is called a
    a. common meringue.
    b. Italian meringue.
    c. French meringue.
    d. Swiss meringue.

Fill in the Blank

1. When preparing an Italian meringue, use a hot sugar syrup that has been heated to

   _____.

2. When preparing a Swiss meringue, combine the egg whites and sugar in a mixing bowl and heat over simmering water to _____ to dissolve the sugar.

2. Heavy cream used for sauces or to lighten mousses should be whipped to _____ stage. When used to cover cakes or tortes, it should be whipped to _____ stage.

3. When separating eggs, to prepare whipped egg whites, you will need _____ well-cleaned containers.

5. The three types of leaveners are _____, _____, and _____.

Matching

_____ 1. organic leavener   _____ 4. physical leavener

_____ 2. stabilizer   _____ 5. chemical leavener

_____ 3. shortener

a. baking soda

b. baking fats

c. yeast

d. steam

e. flour

_____ 1. sourdough starter   _____ 4. gelatin

_____ 2. gluten   _____ 5. crumb

_____ 3. tenderizer   _____ 6. caramel

a. baking fats

b. texture of baked goods

c. wild yeast

d. thickener used in baking

e. protein in flour

f. melted sugar

Written/Short Answer

1. Discuss how to prepare pans for baking.

    _____

    _____

    _____

    _____

2. Discuss how to cool and store baked goods.

    _____

    _____

    _____

    _____

3. What is scaling and why do you do it?

    _____

    _____

    _____

    _____

4. What are the two ways to check for temperature when cooking sugar?

    _____

    _____

    _____

    _____

5. Why and how are ingredients sifted?

    _____

    _____

    _____

    _____

6. What are the three methods for preparing making meringues and when is each used?

    _____

    _____

7. How do you separate eggs?

_____

_____

_____

_____

Essay

1. Discuss the various roles of eggs in the bakeshop.

2. Discuss the various roles of flour in the bakeshop.

CHAPTER **32**

Chapter Overview

An excellent yeast-raised dough requires not only the correct formula and good technique during mixing, kneading, proofing, shaping, and baking.

Chapter Objectives

After reading and studying this chapter, you will be able to

➢ name two basic categories of yeast doughs and describe them

➢ select and prepare ingredients and equipment used to prepare yeast doughs

➢ prepare a yeast dough

➢ scale and shape prepared dough to produce loaves, rolls, and other shapes

➢ evaluate the quality of baked yeasted items according to the proper quality standards

Study Outline

Yeast-raised Dough

Key Terms and Concepts

bake	mix	shape
baker's percentage	oven spring	sourdough
clearing the side of the bowl	pan proofing	sponge method
enriched dough	peel	steam-generating ovens
first fermentation	proof/proofing	straight dough mixing
flatbread	proof box	method
formula	rise/rising	viability of yeast
knead	scale	yeast
lean dough	score	yeast-raised dough
leavened bread	serrated bread knife	

234

Basic Method

Select and prepare the ingredients and equipment

1. Combine the water and yeast in the bowl of an electric mixer.
2. Add all the remaining ingredients to the yeast mixture.
3. Mix until the dough starts to cohere into a ball. Knead the dough until it develops a smooth, elastic texture.
4. Let the dough rise until nearly doubled or tripled, what is known as the first fermentation.
5. Fold the dough over, turn it out of the bowl onto a floured work surface, and scale into pieces.
6. Shape the dough before baking and place in or on prepared pans or molds. Apply eggwash (optional) and proof the dough.
7. Score the bread and bake at the appropriate temperature until baked through.
8. Cool the bread on a rack before slicing and serving or before storing for later service.
9. Evaluate the quality of the bread.

Chapter 32 Exercises

True/False

Indicate whether each of the following statements is True (T) or False(F)

_____ 1. If steam-generating ovens are not available, the effect can be simulated by spraying or brushing the loaves with water.

_____ 2. To achieve a very crisp crust, bread should be baked in dry heat ovens

_____ 3. Yeast-raised breads should not be cut until they have cooled thoroughly.

_____ 4. Doughs that have been brushed with egg wash or milk have a more tender crust than others.

_____ 5. The higher the proportion of eggs and shorteners, the more tender the finished bread.

_____ 6. The formula for the classic French brioche is flour, yeast, salt, and water.

_____ 7. Because it is lacking tenderizers, lean dough is softer and a little more difficult to work with than enriched dough.

_____ 8. The best way to determine doneness of enriched dough breads is with an instant read thermometer.

_____ 9. Once the dough is scaled, it should be rounded into balls and allowed to rest briefly before shaping.

_____ 10. When scaling the dough, each piece is weighed to make sure that all rolls or loaves are the same size.

Multiple Choice

1. Brioche is an example of which type of dough?
   a. Unleavened
   b. Flatbread
   c. Enriched
   d. Lean

2. Pizza dough is most often an example of which type of dough?
   a. Unleavened
   b. Flatbread
   c. Enriched
   d. Lean

3. Sourdough is a type of
   a. shortener.
   b. organic leavener.
   c. tenderizer.
   d. unleavened dough.

4. An enriched dough is produced by
   a. the addition of tenderizing ingredients.
   b. the addition of yeast.
   c. allowing the dough to grow until doubled or tripled in size.
   d. the addition of flavorings, such as nuts or fruit.

5. In order for compressed or fresh yeast to grow properly, water, milk, or other liquids used in bread formula should fall within a temperature range of
   a. 40 to 45°F/4 to 6°C.
   b. 68 to 76°F/20 to 24°C.
   c. 105 to 110°F/40 to 43°C.
   d. 120 to 125°F/49 to 52°C.

Fill in the Blank

1. The formula, or _____, for bread dough is when the basic ingredients are expressed as percentages of the flour.

2. The four essential ingredients for lean dough are _____ , _____ , _____ , and _____ .

3. Breads made from _____ contain only a small amount of sugar and fat. _____ is produced by the addition of fat or tenderizing ingredients such as sugar, butter, or eggs.

4. Letting the dough rise until nearly doubled or tripled, after kneading, is what is known as the _____ .

5. The earliest breads made by blending meals and water and baking in ovens or on griddles were known as _____ . _____ became possible when it was discovered that certain wheats would ferment and rise during baking.

Matching

_____ 1. scale   _____ 4. peel
_____ 2. score   _____ 5. proof
_____ 3. oven spring   _____ 6. formula

a. the final rise of the dough as it bakes
b. baker's percentage
c. to cut the dough into even sized pieces
d. to slash the dough to allow steam to escape during baking
e. tool used to transfer the dough onto the oven rack
f. to test the viability of the yeast

_____ 1. pan proofing   _____ 4. sourdough
_____ 2. first fermentation   _____ 5. knead
_____ 3. baker's percentage

a. natural fermentation occurring in wheat
b. final rise of the dough before baking
c. letting the dough rise until doubled or tripled after kneading
d. formula for bread preparation
e. mixing to develop the strands of gluten

Written/Short Answer

1. What is a baker's percentage?

_____

_____

_____

_____

2. What are some basic and optional tools and equipment needed for preparing and baking yeast-raised dough?

_____

_____

_____

_____

3. What are the differences between lean and enriched dough?

_____

_____

_____

_____

4. When and how should yeast be tested before using?

_____

_____

_____

_____

5. How should pans be prepared for bread baking?

_____

_____

_____

_____

6. Why and how is dough kneaded?

_____

_____

_____

_____

7. How does rising/or proofing affect the finished bread?

_____

_____

_____

_____

Essay

1. Briefly describe how to prepare yeast-raised bread.

2. Explain how to evaluate the quality of yeast-raised breads.

CHAPTER **33**

QUICK BREADS, CAKES, AND OTHER BATTERS

Chapter Overview

Quick breads and cakes differ from yeast breads in that they are based on a batter, rather than a dough. Batters tend to be pourable (with the exception of biscuits and similar quick breads). Batter for cakes and quickbreads often include butter or oil, eggs, and milk or other liquids. The end result is a smooth mixture. When these batters are baked, a tender and delicate texture is formed to produce a wide range of products: muffins, biscuits, and scones are all examples of breakfast pastries made from batters. Simple cakes, such as pound cake and sponge cake, are also made from batters. The baker or pastry chef can enhance these simple items with a wide range of icings, glazes, fillings, and garnishes.

Chapter Objectives

After reading and studying this chapter, you will be able to

➢ name the basic mixing methods for a variety of quick breads, cakes, and other batters

➢ select and prepare ingredients and equipment for each of the following mixing methods: straight mix, rubbed dough, creaming, foaming

➢ categorize baked goods such as cakes, muffins, biscuits according to their mixing method

➢ evaluate the quality of finished baked items according to the proper quality characteristics

➢ select and use the appropriate ingredients, preparations, and equipment in order to prepare assembled cakes

Study Outline

The Straight-Mix Method

Key Terms and Concepts

blend	fold	pastry flour
chemical leaveners	organic leaveners	straight-mix method

Basic Method

Select and prepare the ingredients and equipment

1. Sift the dry ingredients together.
2. Combine the liquid ingredients in a bowl.
3. Add the combined liquid ingredients to the combined dry ingredients.
4. Scale the batter into baking pans, popover pans, ramekins, a crêpe pan, or griddle.
5. Bake or cook the batter.
6. Evaluate the quality of the finished item.

Rubbed-Dough Method

Key Terms and Concepts

laminate
rubbed-dough method
working the dough, fat, and so on

Basic Method

Select and prepare the ingredients and equipment

1. Combine the dry ingredients in a bowl and blend.
2. Rub cold butter or other shortening into the dry ingredients.
3. Add the liquid ingredients and blend into a dough.
4. Transfer the dough onto a floured work surface and gather it into a ball.
5. (Optional) Fold and roll the dough to laminate it.
6. Scale and shape the dough, place on prepared pans, and bake or cook until done.
7. Evaluate the quality of the finished item.

The Creaming Method

Key Terms and Concepts

alternating sequence   creaming method
creaming   paddle attachment

Basic Method

Select and prepare the ingredients and equipment

1. Sift the dry ingredients together.
2. Cream together the fat and sugar and blend them on medium speed until the mixture is smooth, light, and creamy.
3. Gradually add the eggs to the creamed mixture.
4. Add the sifted dry ingredients, alternating with the liquid ingredients, if any, on low speed. Mix until the batter is very smooth.
5. Scale off the batter into prepared baking pans and bake at the appropriate temperature until done.
6. Evaluate the quality of the finished item.

The Foaming Method

Key Terms and Concepts

foam
foaming method
meringue
simmering water bath
sponge

Basic Method

Select and prepare the ingredients and equipment

1. Sift the dry ingredients together.
2. Combine the eggs and sugar.
3. Warm foaming method
4. Cold foaming method
5. Beat the eggs and sugar to a foam.
6. Gently fold in the sifted dry ingredients.
7. Add other ingredients, such as butter, flavoring, or finishing ingredients.
8. Scale off the batter into prepared baking pans and bake until done.
9. Evaluate the quality of the finished product.

General Guidelines for Assembling Cakes

Chapter 33 Exercises

True/False

Indicate whether each of the following statements is True (T) or False(F)

_____ 1.   For the foaming method, the eggs and sugar are always warmed over a simmering water bath.

_____ 2.   For the foaming method, the dry ingredients should always be folded into the foam by hand.

_____ 3.   In general, the straight-mix method and the creaming method can be used interchangeably.

_____ 4.   Biscuits and muffins are both made using the creaming method.

_____ 5.   Some muffins and quick breads prepared by the straight-mix method normally develop a crack on their crust when baking.

_____ 6.   Whole eggs may be used to prepare the foam for an item mixed by the foaming method.

_____ 7.   When preparing items by the rubbed-dough method, the ingredients should all be at room temperature to achieve the best consistency.

_____ 8.   When using the foaming method, the butter should be chilled before being added to the foam so that it doesn't deflate the delicate batter.

_____ 9.   Eggs, sugar, and flour are the principal components of a foam cake.

_____ 10.   Muffins can be prepared using the straight-mix method or the creaming method.

Multiple Choice

1.   To prepare a batter by the foaming method:
   a.   Blend the fat and sugar until smooth and light. Gradually add the eggs. Add the combined sifted dry ingredients.
   b.   Beat the eggs and sugar together to form a ribbon. Gently fold in the dry ingredients. Add other ingredients.

c. Combine all the liquid ingredients in a bowl. Add the liquid ingredients to the combined sifted dry ingredients.

d. Combine the dry ingredients in a bowl. Work cold butter or other shortening into the dry ingredients. Add liquid ingredients and blend.

2. To prepare a batter by the straight-mix method:

a. Blend the fat and sugar until smooth and light. Gradually add the eggs. Add the combined sifted dry ingredients.

b. Beat the eggs and sugar together to form a ribbon. Gently fold in the dry ingredients. Add other ingredients.

c. Combine all the liquid ingredients in a bowl. Add the liquid ingredients to the combined sifted dry ingredients.

d. Combine the dry ingredients in a bowl. Work cold butter or other shortening into the dry ingredients. Add liquid ingredients and blend.

3. To prepare a batter by the rubbed-dough method:

a. Blend the fat and sugar until smooth and light. Gradually add the eggs. Add the combined sifted dry ingredients.

b. Beat the eggs and sugar together to form a ribbon. Gently fold in the dry ingredients. Add other ingredients.

c. Combine all the liquid ingredients in a bowl. Add the liquid ingredients to the combined sifted dry ingredients.

d. Combine the dry ingredients in a bowl. Work cold butter or other shortening into the dry ingredients. Add liquid ingredients and blend.

4. To prepare a batter by the creaming method:

a. Blend the fat and sugar until smooth and light. Gradually add the eggs. Add the combined sifted dry ingredients.

b. Beat the eggs and sugar together to form a ribbon. Gently fold in the dry ingredients. Add other ingredients.

c. Combine all the liquid ingredients in a bowl. Add the liquid ingredients to the combined sifted dry ingredients.

d. Combine the dry ingredients in a bowl. Work cold butter or other shortening into the dry ingredients. Add liquid ingredients and blend.

5. Angel food cake is an example of an item prepared by the

a. straight-mix method.
b. rubbed-dough method.
c. foaming method.
d. creaming method.

Fill in the Blank

1. In the _____ method, the fat is kept very cold to inhibit it from easily blending with the flour.

2. For the warm foaming method, the eggs and sugar should be warmed _____
   _____.

3. Muffins can be prepared using the _____ method or the _____ method.

4. Pancakes are typically made using the _____ method.

5. Chiffon cakes and madeleines are made using the _____ method.

Matching

_____ 1. fold   _____ 4. scale
_____ 2. muffin   _____ 5. sponge
_____ 3. scone   _____ 6. meringue

a. baked item prepared by rubbed-dough method
b. to stir a light mixture into a heavier mixture
c. whipped egg whites and sugar
d. baked item prepared by creaming method
e. texture/crumb produced by foaming method
f. portion the batter before baking

_____ 1. cream   _____ 4. foam
_____ 2. laminate   _____ 5. crêpe
_____ 3. genoise

a. baked item prepared by foaming method
b. item prepared by straight-mix method
c. egg whites and sugar beaten to form a ribbon
d. blend fat and sugar together until smooth
e. fold the dough like a letter or book

Written/Short Answer

1. Briefly explain the straight-mix method.

_____

_____

_____

_____

2. Briefly explain the rubbed-dough method.

_____

_____

_____

_____

3. Briefly explain the creaming method.

_____

_____

_____

_____

4. Briefly explain the foaming method.

_____

_____

_____

_____

5. What are the two methods of creating a foam?

_____

_____

_____

_____

6. What precautions must be taken when preparing an item by the foaming method?

_____

_____

_____

_____

7. What precautions must be taken when preparing an item by the rubbed-dough method?

_____

_____

Essay

1. What are the general guidelines for assembling cakes?

2. What are the tools used for assembling cakes?

CHAPTER 34

PASTRY DOUGHS AND COOKIES

Chapter Overview

All chefs should be able to prepare and work with a variety of doughs to prepare both sweet and savory items ranging from pastries, pies and cookies. The same pie crust, for example, can be paired with sweetened fresh for an apple pie or with a cheese-flavored custard to make quiche. Individually-sized pastries and cookies may be served outside a meal, as hors d'oeuvre or reception food, or to conclude the meal as a friandise or mignardise. Or they may be featured as a part of the regular menu offerings as an entrée, an appetizer, or a dessert.

Chapter Objectives

After reading and studying this chapter, you will be able to

➢ name the basic mixing methods for a variety of pastry doughs and cookies

➢ select and prepare ingredients and equipment for each of the following: basic pie dough, laminated doughs, and pâte à choux

➢ name a variety of mixing and shaping methods used to produce the following cookie types: scooped and dropped, rolled and cut, molded an dslice (or icebox), biscotti, piped, and stenciled

➢ describe the procedures for working with, shaping, filling, and baking a variety of items prepared with pastry doughs

➢ evaluate the quality of pastries and cookies according to the proper quality characteristics

Study Outline

Basic Pie Dough

Key Terms and Concepts

3-2-1 dough	blind baking	pie
flaky	docking	pie weights
lattice	double panning	tart
mealy	pâte sucrée	

Basic Method

Select and prepare the ingredients and equipment

1. Combine the flour and the fat.
2. Add the cold water to the dough and combine.
3. Roll out the dough.
4. Line the pie or tart pan with the dough.
5. Finish and fill the pie crust as desired.
6. Bake the pie or pie crust.
7. Evaluate the quality of the finished pie or crust.

Blind Baking

Laminated Doughs

Key Terms and Concepts

blitz puff pastry	laminate	puff pastry
croissant	locking the roll-in in place	roll-in
Danish	marking the dough	three-fold
four-fold	pâte feuilletée	

Basic Method

Select and prepare the ingredients and equipment

Make the laminated dough
1. Combine the ingredients for the dough and knead.
2. Mix the roll-in.
3. Combine the dough and the roll-in and lock the roll-in in place.
4. Laminate the dough by turning, rolling, and folding it.
   - Keep the dough chilled, taking out only the amount to be worked with at a given moment.
   - Use a sharp knife when shaping or cutting the dough.
   - Do not run the rolling pin over the edge of the dough; this will destroy the layers at the edges and cause the dough to rise unevenly.
   - Refrigerate puff pastry before baking.
   - Save puff pastry scraps.
5. Evaluate the quality of the finished product.

Phyllo Dough

Pâte à choux

Key Terms and Concepts

cream puffs	pâte à choux	gougère
éclair	profiteroles	

Basic Method

Select and prepare the ingredients and equipment

1. Bring the liquid and butter to a full boil. Add the flour and cook, stirring constantly.
2. Add the eggs.
3. Portion and bake the dough.
4. Evaluate the quality of the finished item.

Guidelines for Shaping and Baking Cookies

➢ Scooped and dropped cookies

➢ Rolled and cut cookies

➢ Molded and sliced cookies

➢ Biscotti

➢ Piped cookies

➢ Stenciled cookies

Chapter 34 Exercises

True/False

Indicate whether each of the following statements is True (T) or False(F)

_____ 1. Stenciled cookies are made from a stiff batter that is usually chilled before using.

_____ 2. Icebox or molded and sliced cookies are typically used to prepare tuiles and cookie "cups."

_____ 3. Rolled cookies should generally be cut no more than 1/8 to 1/6 in / 2 to 4 mm thick.

_____ 4. When preparing the pâte à choux batter, the eggs should be tempered before they are added to the boiling liquid, butter, and flour.

_____ 5. Puff pastry is a precooked batter that expands to a hollow shell when baked.

_____ 6. Double panning is the procedure used when baking the top crust separately from the bottom crust.

_____ 7. When rolling out basic pie dough, start in the middle and do not allow the rolling pin to go all the way to the edge.

_____ 8. When a crust is prebaked by the double panning method, the crust is baked upside down.

_____ 9. If milk or cream is used in a 3-2-1 dough, the amount of fat in the formula should be reduced.

_____ 10. The characteristic flaky texture of baked pie dough is developed by blending the fat and flour into a smooth dough.

Multiple Choice

1. 3-2-1 dough is so called because it is
   a. 3 parts fat, 2 parts flour, 1 part water.
   b. 3 parts flour, 2 parts fat, 1 part water.
   c. 3 pounds flour, 2 pounds fat, 1 cup water.
   d. made in three simple steps.

2. In a basic pie dough, once the flour, fat, and liquid have been combined,
   a. knead the dough to develop the gluten.
   b. roll out the dough and bake.
   c. chill the dough.
   d. laminate the dough.

3. For a double crusted pie, brush with egg wash, and bake at
   a. 350°F/175°C.
   b. 375°F/190°C.
   c. 425°F/220°C.
   d. 450°F/230°C.

4. When baking pâte à choux, the starting temperature should be
   a. 350 to 375°F/175 to 190°C.
   b. 375 to 400°F/190 to 205°C.

c. 400 to 425°F/205 to 220°C.
d. 425 to 450°F/220 to 230°C.

5. Scooped and dropped cookies are usually baked at
   a. 325 to 350°F/165 to 175°C.
   b. 350 to 375°F/175 to 190°C.
   c. 375 to 400°F/190 to 205°C.
   d. 400 to 425°F/205 to 220°C.

Fill in the Blank

1. _____dough, usually used to prepare strudel and baklava, is composed of flour and water, and occasionally oil.

2. In a 3-2-1-dough, large pieces of fat make a _____pie dough. If the fat is worked more thoroughly into the flour, the result will be a pie crust with a small flake, or _____dough.

3. Basic pie dough is known as _____. Adding sugar to the basic formula produces a dough known as _____.

4. The _____for laminated doughs is made from butter or a combination of butter and shortening, and sometimes flour.

5. A _____is made by cutting strips of dough and laying them on the top of the pie to make a grid.

Matching

_____ 1. docking
_____ 2. laminating
_____ 3. croissant

_____ 4. double panning
_____ 5. pâte sucrée
_____ 6. profiterole

a. method of blind baking
b. combining a basic dough with a roll-in
c. piercing the dough before prebaking a pie shell
d. prepared from pâte à choux
e. prepared from enriched laminated dough
f. sweetened pie dough

_____ 1. pâte feuilletée
_____ 2. 3-2-1 dough
_____ 3. pâte à choux

_____ 4. roll-in
_____ 5. blind baking

a. an additional layer of butter in laminated dough
b. a precooked batter that puffs when baked
c. prebaking a pie or tart shell
d. puff pastry
e. pie dough

Written/Short Answer

1. Briefly describe the method for preparing a pie or tart crust.

_____

_____

_____

_____

2. What are some types of toppings for pies and tarts?

_____

_____

_____

_____

3. What is blind baking; why and how is it done?

_____

_____

_____

_____

4. Briefly describe the method for preparing a laminated dough.

_____

_____

_____

_____

5. Briefly describe the method for preparing and baking pâte à choux.

_____

6. How is pâte à choux used once it is baked?

_____

_____

_____

_____

7. What is phyllo? How is it used?

_____

_____

_____

_____

Essay

1. What are some general guidelines and precautions for working with laminated doughs?

2. What are some basic types of cookies and give some guidelines for preparing each.

CHAPTER **35**

ICINGS, DESSERT SAUCES, AND CREAMS

Chapter Overview

The difference between a plain baked item and a fancy pastry often relies on the presence of an icing or filling, a sauce, or a glaze. The ability to prepare a number of basic sauces and creams makes it possible to give basic cakes a great deal of variety without a great deal of effort.

Chapter Objectives

After reading and studying this chapter, you will be able to

➢ name four types of buttercream and list their basic ingredients

➢ select and prepare ingredients and equipment for buttercreams, vanilla sauce, pasty cream, Bavarian creams, and mousse

➢ name several applications for vanilla sauce and pastry cream

➢ select and prepare ingredients and equipment for ganache

➢ name several applications for ganache

➢ work with fondant correctly to apply it as a glaze or coating

➢ apply the general guidelines for icings, sauces, and glazes to produce finished desserts and pastries

Study Outline

Buttercream

Key Terms and Concepts

common meringue	Italian buttercream	sugar syrup
French buttercream	Italian meringue	Swiss buttercream
German buttercream	pastry cream	

Basic Method

Select and prepare the ingredients and equipment

Make the buttercream
1. Prepare the base for the buttercream.
2. Combine the syrup and the egg whites.
3. Gradually add softened butter to the base and beat the mixture until a smooth, light buttercream is formed.
4. Evaluate the quality of the buttercream.

Vanilla Sauce

Key Terms and Concepts

Bavarian cream	frozen soufflé	sauce anglaise
custard	ice cream	temper
custard sauce	parfait	vanilla sauce

Basic Method

Select and prepare the ingredients and equipment

Make the vanilla sauce
1. Combine the milk with half of the sugar (and the vanilla bean, if using) and bring to a simmer.
2. Combine the egg yolks or eggs with the remaining sugar in a stainless steel bowl.
3. Combine the hot milk or cream mixture with the eggs.
4. Strain the sauce and cool the sauce.
5. Evaluate the quality of the finished sauce or custard.

Pastry Cream

Key Terms and Concepts

crème pâtisserie	soufflé base
pastry cream	vanilla sauce

Basic Method

Select and prepare the ingredients and equipment

Make the pastry cream
1. Combine the milk with half of the sugar (and the vanilla bean, if using) and bring to the boiling point.
2. Blend the remaining sugar and cornstarch and add the eggs. Temper the egg mixture with some of the hot milk.
3. Add the butter and flavorings if not using a vanilla bean.
4. Evaluate the quality of the finished pastry cream.

Bavarian Cream

Key Terms and Concepts

Bavarian cream
bloom
frozen soufflé

gel point
gelatin
parfait

stabilize

Basic Method

Select and prepare the ingredients

Make the Bavarian cream
1. Combine the vanilla sauce with bloomed gelatin and any flavoring ingredients.
2. Cool the base to 75°F/24°C over an ice bath.
3. Fold in the whipped cream gently but thoroughly. The Bavarian is ready to mold and chill (or freeze) for later service.
4. Evaluate the quality of the finished Bavarian cream.

Mousse

Key Terms and Concepts

foam
mousse

Basic Method

Select and prepare the ingredients and equipment

Make the mousse
1. Prepare the flavor ingredients for the mousse and cool.
2. Heat the egg yolks and sugar to 145°F/63°C for 15 seconds, whisking constantly.
3. Beat the egg whites with the remaining sugar to stiff peaks and fold the egg whites into the egg yolk mixture.
4. Fold the flavoring ingredients and whipped cream into the egg mixture.
5. Evaluate the quality of the finished mousse.

Ganache

Key Terms and Concepts

ganache
glaze
hard ganache
light ganache
truffles

Basic Method

Select and prepare the ingredients and equipment

Make the ganache
1. Combine the cream and chocolate.
2. Stir the mixture until the chocolate is completely melted.
3. Evaluate the quality of the finished sauce.

General guidelines for Icings, Glazes, and Sauces

Key Terms and Concepts

Bavarian cream
buttercream
chantilly cream
diplomat cream
fondant

ganache
glaze
mousse
seal-coat
seed method

tempered chocolate
truffles
whipped cream

Icings and fillings for cakes and pastries

Dessert sauces

Tempering fondant and glazing

Glazing cakes, cookies, or pastries with ganache

Making truffles

Tempering Chocolate

1. Chop the chocolate with a serrated knife and put it in a stainless steel bowl. Place the bowl over very low heat or barely simmering water, making sure than no moisture comes in contact with the chocolate. Stir the chocolate occasionally as it melts to keep it at an even temperature throughout.
2. Continue to heat the chocolate until it reaches a temperature between 105 and 110°F/40 and 43°C. Use an instant-read thermometer for the most accurate results.
3. Remove the chocolate from the heat. Add a large piece of unmelted chocolate (the seed) and stir it until the temperature drops to 87 to 92°F/30 to 33°C. If the chocolate drops below 85°F/29°C, it will be necessary to repeat the steps described here to gently reheat it to 92°F/33°C. If the chocolate scorches or becomes grainy, it can no longer be used. If any moisture comes in contact with the chocolate as it is being tempered it will seize.

Chapter 35 Exercises

True/False

Indicate whether each of the following statements is True (T) or False(F)

_____ 1. Pastry cream is often used as a base for sweet soufflés.

_____ 2. Frozen vanilla sauce is better known as a frozen soufflé.

_____ 3. When using a vanilla bean to flavor custard or pastry cream, the seeds should be removed and discarded before adding the pod.

_____ 4. When preparing buttercreams, the butter should be thoroughly chilled when it is added to the base.

_____ 5. Buttercreams typically call for granulated sugar, which should be sifted if necessary.

_____ 6. Mousses are generally prepared with a foam of whipped egg whites and/or whipped cream.

_____ 7. The desired consistency of a finished vanilla sauce will be determined by its intended use.

_____ 8. The desired consistency of a finished ganache will be determined by its intended use.

_____ 9. When preparing an Italian buttercream, the cooked sugar syrup should be beaten into egg whites whipped to medium peaks.

_____ 10. Buttercreams begin to lose their volume once prepared, and should be used immediately.

Multiple Choice

1. Italian buttercream begins with a base of
   a. a common meringue.
   b. a room temperature pastry cream beaten until smooth and light.
   c. yolks and sugar heated to 145°F/63°C.
   d. sugar syrup cooked to the softball stage and then whipped with egg whites.

2. German buttercream begins with a base of
   a. a common meringue.
   b. a room temperature pastry cream beaten until smooth and light.
   c. yolks and sugar heated to 145°F/63°C.
   d. sugar syrup cooked to the softball stage and then whipped with egg whites.

3. Swiss buttercream begins with a base of
   a. common meringue.
   b. a room temperature pastry cream beaten until smooth and light.
   c. yolks and sugar heated to 145°F/63°C.
   d. sugar syrup cooked to the softball stage and then whipped with egg whites.

4. French buttercream begins with a base of
   a. a common meringue.
   b. a room temperature pastry cream beaten until smooth and light.
   c. yolks and sugar heated to 145°F/63°C.
   d. sugar syrup cooked to the softball stage and then whipped with egg whites.

5. When a gelatin stabilizer is added to vanilla sauce, it produces
   a. sauce anglaise.
   b. Bavarian cream.
   c. buttercream.
   d. pastry cream.

Fill in the Blank

1. A vanilla sauce stabilized with whipped cream and gelatin added produces _____. Before adding the gelatin, it must be _____.

2. Two preparations discussed in this chapter that are typically used to glaze cakes or petit fours are _____ and _____.

4. Pastry cream is cooked in a non-reactive saucepan such as stainless steel to avoid _____.

4. The primary ingredients of vanilla sauce are _____, _____ and _____.

5. The primary ingredients of ganache are _____ and _____.

Matching

_____ 1. pastry cream   _____ 4. chantilly cream

_____ 2. vanilla sauce   _____ 5. temper

_____ 3. ganache   _____ 6. bloom

a. to soften gelatin
b. sauce anglaise
c. heated cream and chocolate
d. to warm chocolate or fondant until liquid
e. crème pâtisserie
f. whipped heavy cream

_____ 1. Bavarian cream   _____ 4. buttercream

_____ 2. truffles   _____ 5. fondant

_____ 3. mousse

a. flavored dessert stabilized with whipped cream and/or eggs
b. a sugar glaze
c. vanilla sauce stabilized with gelatin

d. confection made from hard ganache

e. a rich filling usually prepared with a meringue base

Written/Short Answer

1. Briefly describe the four types of buttercream and explain the differences. What are they used for?

_____

_____

_____

_____

2. Briefly describe the technique for preparing Italian buttercream.

_____

_____

_____

_____

3. Briefly describe how to make a vanilla sauce. What is it used for?

_____

_____

_____

_____

4. Briefly describe how to make pastry cream. What is it used for?

_____

_____

_____

_____

5. Briefly describe how to make Bavarian cream. What is it used for?

_____

_____

_____

6. Briefly describe how to make mousse. What is it used for?

_____

_____

_____

_____

7. Briefly describe how to make ganache and what is it used for?

_____

_____

_____

_____

Essay

1. Discuss the general guidelines for icing and glazing desserts.

2. Discuss how dessert sauces are used in the professional kitchen.

3. How do you temper fondant and chocolate and what are they used for?